Construction management in developing countries

ENGINEERING MANAGEMENT

Series editor S. H. Wearne, BSc(Eng), PhD, CEng, FICE, Consultant, Director of Institution courses and in-company training

Editorial panel D. E. Neale, CEng, FICE; D. P. Maguire, BSc, CEng, FICE; D. J. Ricketts, BSc, CEng, MICE; J. V. Tagg, CEng, FICE; J. C. Bircumshaw, BSc, CEng, MICE

Other titles in the series

ENGINEERING MANAGEMENT

Construction management in developing countries

EurIng R. K. Loraine, BSc, CEng, FICE, FFB, FBIM

 Thomas Telford, London

Published by Thomas Telford Ltd, Thomas Telford House, 1 Heron Quay, London E14 4JD

First published 1992

British Library Cataloguing in Publication Data
Loraine, R. K.
    Construction management in developing countries.
    I. Title
    624.068

ISBN: 0 7277 1651 4

Typeset in Great Britain by MHL Typesetting Limited, Coventry
Printed and bound in Great Britain by Billing and Sons Ltd, Worcester

Contents

Introduction

This book is intended to address the special problems of managing construction projects outside the UK. As these problems vary considerably from country to country, it was decided to concentrate on the developing world, as it is here that the differences from working in the UK are most marked.

The problems are essentially caused by remoteness from a home base, lack of facilities available locally, maintenance of long lines of communication and supply, and mobilization of large-scale resources in relatively unknown territories. These are all addressed in the following chapters.

The foreign strategy of the large Western contractors has radically changed in the past few years. There is now a greater emphasis on working in economically developed territories. The biggest change has been the winding-down of local subsidiaries in the developing world, due to reduced work-load, lack of convertible funds and strong local competition, which is often uncommercial.

Such work as is acquired now in developing countries is therefore likely to be on a project basis. This involves setting up purely for the contract in hand. Without having local subsidiaries to provide continuity of experience, knowledge of a country and area has to be extensively updated for each project, and mobilization may have to be carried out without local support.

This book does not deal with projects that are contractor promoted. Projects are mostly funded by multilateral or bilateral agencies. Other than in a few credit-worthy countries, funding solely from a client's own resources is unreliable with regard to both convertibility and amount and is unlikely to be acceptable to international contractors. Comment is therefore made on relationships with, and the requirements of, the lending agencies.

The pattern of the book is illustrated in Fig. 1. Whereas the emphasis is on the management of construction, a description is also given of how projects are secured, as this influences the style of management.

A substantial section of the book is devoted to security. This

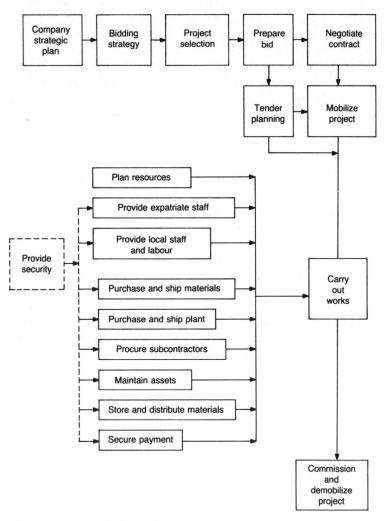

Fig. 1. Pattern of the book

involves the protection of both physical resources and expatriate staff. Because of extended supply lines, losses of materials or plant can have a much more severe impact on the progress of works than at home, and proportionally greater efforts must be made to reduce the possibility of such occurrences. Of even greater concern is the safety of expatriate staff and their dependants.

Security in the sense of making provision for a client's failure to pay is also referred to. Notwithstanding the comment above on activities being restricted to credit-worthy countries, circumstances can change and non-payment risks can arise. Fig. 1 illustrates how security and executive activities interrelate.

The recruitment of European expatriates to Third World projects is becoming increasingly difficult. Recent events have brought into prominence the security aspects of working in such countries. A well constructed security plan is necessary to provide comfort when recruiting staff. However, it is hoped that this emphasis on security does not give the book a negative flavour. Working in developing countries is uniquely rewarding and will always appeal to the more adventurous.

The construction industry has progressively become more structured and home office controlled and it is only on a Third World assignment that a project manager can have anything like the old-time authority of the company's 'agent'. To achieve this successfully requires a positive approach to security and in this it is hoped that the book can be of use.

The book does not promote theories of management but is confined to the tools used in the management of resources. There may appear to some repetition between sections. This is the result of trying to provide, within each section, a check-list of those activities that are relevant to the stage of the project being discussed.

1 Selecting bidding opportunities

This chapter considers the formulation and application of a bidding strategy, and the generation of bidding criteria.

Bidding strategy

The process by which a British contractor acquires work overseas should start with the formulation of a bidding strategy; this, in turn, leads to the identification of opportunities. The process is shown in Fig. 2. The objectives of the bidding strategy should be set by the company strategic plan.

The marketing effort required to follow up project opportunities in the developing world consumes both time and resources. The bidding strategy must therefore be very selective. As there is unlikely to be a commitment to a specific territory where there is a local presence, a large amount of information must be processed to formulate the bidding strategy, and a mechanism has to be set up to sift and select this information.

The selection criteria for this mechanism are likely to be

- product type: a detailed description of the type of work sought

- geographical interest: territories where advantages are perceived

- 'no-go' areas: politically or commercially unacceptable territories or clients

- partners and associates: companies with joint or complementary interests, usually where there is a history of co-operation; in certain cases, complementary national characteristics, possibly associated with financing or political advantages

- UK advantages: territories or clients where a British connection is an advantage — political or financial.

5

To process this information effectively, procedures are needed

- to set a budget for the marketing activity
- to allocate resources to it
- to prepare marketing data, including publicity, contact lists, pre-qualification documentation, client information and business volume projections

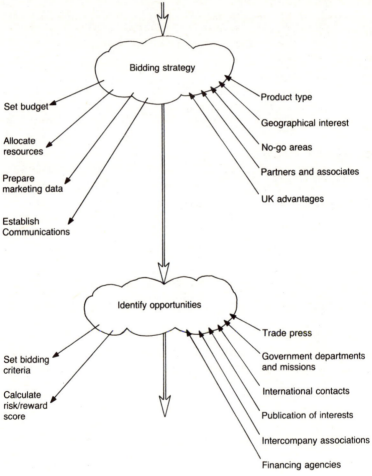

Fig. 2. Process for acquiring work overseas

6

- to establish communications, including scheduling visits, seminars, publicity campaigns and presentations, accompanying UK Government officials, inviting key client representatives to visit and making local contacts and agents in preferred territories.

These activities should result in the identification of individual opportunities, which are then subjected to selection procedures.

Bidding criteria

Compliance with a strict set of bidding criteria must be ensured. Such criteria may concern

- competition
- number of bidders
- conditions of contract
- quality of bidding documents
- resource restraints
- guarantees and penalties
- bidding time
- construction period
- special opportunities: contacts, alternative designs etc.

These criteria should be analysed in detail against subjective and objective standards and should also be processed through some form of risk/reward scoring mechanism which will give notional values to the key bidding criteria. The two forms of analysis should be considered as complementary to each other. The score sheet is merely a means of quickly identifying levels of risk. The decision should not rest solely with achieving a minimum score. There may be good reasons given in the subjective analysis for proceeding with a bid.

2 Acquiring local knowledge

Extensive updating of local knowledge is usually needed when a decision to bid has been made. Increasingly, international contractors curtail their activities in the underdeveloped world to 'hit and run' operations without local continuity. Therefore each opportunity requires a considerable reinforcement of knowledge.

Much information can be obtained without leaving the home base. Some of this should already have been used in making the decision to bid. Sources of this information are shown in Fig. 3.

Check-lists

Before a visit to the country is made, extensive check-lists should be prepared of the information required.

Such check lists should include

- climate
  - seasons
  - rainfall
  - temperature

- natural occurrences
  - storm conditions
  - tectonic movements and disturbances
  - tides
  - flood incidence

- demographic and social structure
  - history of personal liberty and security
  - continuity of governments and institutions
  - language
  - tribal and ethnic divisions
  - population distribution

o age distribution
o towns and cities
o religion
o industries and employment
o local customs

● political, fiscal and legal
o constitution and political parties
o blacklists and political clearances
o levies
o residence permits and visas
o stamp duty
o taxes: particular reference to relationship between taxes and contractual matters and clearance procedures, company,

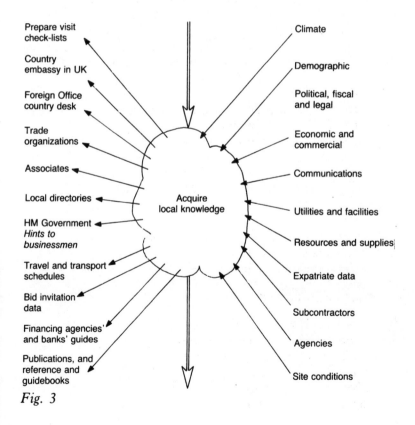

Prepare visit
check-lists

Country
embassy in UK

Foreign Office
country desk

Trade
organizations

Associates

Local directories

HM Government
*Hints to
businessmen*

Travel and transport
schedules

Bid invitation
data

Financing agencies'
and banks' guides

Publications, and
reference and
guidebooks

Acquire
local knowledge

Climate

Demographic

Political, fiscal
and legal

Economic and
commercial

Communications

Utilities and facilities

Resources and supplies

Expatriate data

Subcontractors

Agencies

Site conditions

Fig. 3

individual, payroll, municipal, turnover, vehicle and road, withholding, double taxation relief and other offsets
- o custom and other duties
- o licences
- o insurances
- o police powers
- o relationship between law and contract
- o legal-authority clearance of documents and contracts
- o effectiveness and impartiality of arbitration

- economic and commercial
- o records of inflation
- o escalation provisions
- o currency and rates of exchange
- o hedging provisions
- o exchange controls
- o borrowing limits and procedures
- o documentary credits and bills of exchange
- o banks and finance houses
- o transfer charges
- o audit and other fees
- o contract funding

- communications
- o telephone, telegraph, telex and fax: availability, cost and procedures
- o air, rail and road transport, fare structure and cost
- o airports: facilities and capacities
- o seaports: facilities and capacities
- o port and airport clearance and demurrage
- o route restrictions
- o border crossings and procedures
- o history of port and airport delays
- o security in transit
- o radio: availability, licensing and procedures
- o inland freight rates
- o air charter

- utilities and facilities
- o electricity: load capacity, proximity, tariff, availability, reliability

- o private generation: licence
- o water: availability, reliability, potability, tariff, proximity
- o sewage/refuse
- o gas: availability, proximity, reliability, capacity, tariff mains or bottle supply
- o office and industrial premises

- ● resources and supplies
- o labour and local staff: availability and location
- o labour and staff rates
- o hire and fire regulations and procedures
- o health and safety regulations and welfare
- o medical facilities available
- o tribal and political restrictions
- o holidays
- o transportation, accommodation and feeding
- o importation of labour, and work permits
- o working hours, holidays and overtime
- o social security provisions and cost
- o materials check-list
- o delivery facilities
- o local construction plant available for hire
- o plant and spares sales and back-up: delivery pipeline and security
- o agencies and servicing facilities
- o resale potential
- o fuel and lubricants supply

- ● expatriate support data
- o work permits
- o laws and regulations relating to residents
- o availability of work for dependants
- o medical facilities
- o schooling
- o local transport
- o shopping facilities
- o leisure and entertainment
- o standard shopping basket relating to cost of living
- o transfer-of-funds regulations

- ● subcontractors

11

o availability
o type
o plant hire
o transport
o labour only
o specialist
o general
o size
o local subcontract terms and conditions
o possible client interference on selection of subcontractors
o nature and amount of work in progress in territory

● agents
o local representatives of international suppliers
o laws and regulations relating to representation
o local contacts offered

● site information
o topography
o geology: rock levels etc., availability of fill and topsoil, siting of spoil and borrow pits
o hydrology
o access
o proximity of services

Some of the items in the check-lists can be provisionally completed from information available before the territory is visited. These answers can be checked out during the visit.

When the check-lists have been completed, it may be necessary to reconsider the decision to bid.

Some of the information needed for the bid may be received after completion of the visit, from contacts made during the visit, and should then be added to the summarized data used by the estimator.

3 Preparing a bid

Nowadays the preparation of a bid for a large project in a developing country is not fundamentally different from one at home. The basic techniques are the same. A computerized estimating system can be used with reasonably similar facility. The databank will undoubtedly need to be updated with the major factors of cost for each country, but the number of manual calculations is not dissimilar to that for a major project in the economically developed world.

Because of the distance between the site and head office, the total time needed is greater than for a home bid. A bid for a large project is likely to need at least four months from initial invitation to submission, as shown in Fig. 4. Six months is a more satisfactory period.

Communications in most countries have improved out of all recognition in the past ten years, and once local contacts have been made information can flow by telephone and fax with reasonable ease.

Collection of documents
The collection and transmission of documents is likely to take up to two weeks if partners in different countries are involved. This may involve the use of a local agent to obtain the documents in the first place.

Agreements
In some developing countries the use of a local agent may be mandatory, by government decree. In some it may be illegal. In most it will be advisable. Care must be taken to establish the legal position and level of commission payments. Some form of prebid agreement should to be established at the beginning covering the

14

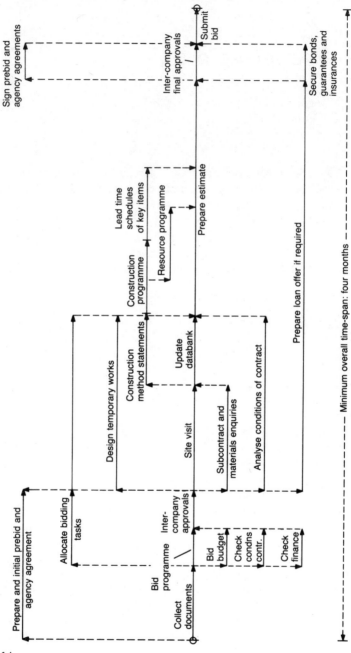

Fig. 4. Programme for bid preparation for a large project

Table 1. Principal terms of an agency agreement

Description of parties to agreement
Intent of Agreement
Definitions
Duties of agent: warranty of performance
Limitations: entire understanding of parties
Confidentiality and exclusivity
   No unauthorized commitments on parties by agent
   No unauthorized disclosures by agent
   Notices
Payment: currencies
Assignment
Law of agreement
Duration of agreement
Termination provisions
   Insolvency
   Breach
   Improper acts
   Termination of principal contract
Arbitration
Schedules to agreement

principal terms, and this should be initialled before bidding documents are purchased, to avoid disputes later. These principal terms are illustrated in Table 1.

If a joint venture between construction companies is proposed, a prebid agreement between them stating all matters of principle should be initialled as soon as possible.

These agreements should be developed progressively during the bidding period and should be signed prior to submission of the tender.

In principle it is advisable to sign a full joint venture agreement at this stage, rather than leave any opening for later dispute. In most cases standard documents are used which require little modification. If for any reason it is impossible to sign the joint venture agreement at this stage, the prebid agreement should have an accepted form of full joint venture agreement attached to it to indicate the scope of the intended eventual agreement. Typical headings for a joint venture agreement are listed in Table 2.

15

In some bids the Client may require that an outline joint venture agreement is included in the tender submission documentation. This should be a specially prepared synopsis of the main terms of the joint venture agreement for the purpose of demonstrating the nature of the association being proposed.

Table 2. Principal terms of a joint venture agreement

Description of parties to agreement
Intent of agreement
Definitions
Participation of parties
Preparation and submission of tender
Acceptance of tender
Bank accounts and provision of working capital
Execution and control of works
    Joint venture board
    Project Manager
    Provision of staff
Construction plant and other assets
Purchases and orders: authority
Payment of fees
Insurances
Services by individual parties: leader
Keeping of accounts of joint venture
Realization of assets
Final accounts of joint venture
Default of parties and remedies
    Insolvency
    Non-payment of working capital
    Breach
Duration of agreement
Confidentiality and exclusivity
    No unauthorized commitments
    No unauthorized disclosures or publicity
Assignment
Arbitration
Law of agreement
Severability: invalidity of individual terms do not affect validity of
    remainder
Schedules of agreement

Reconfirm intention to bid

Although the intent to bid should have been established by the various parties before issue of the invitation, there may be several matters that come to light in the tender documentation that make a reconfirmation of this necessary.

The information that is likely to be included in such a review includes

● bid programme

● bid budget

● conditions of contract

● sources of finance and security of payment

● technical reassessment.

With regard to the sources of finance, it may be that the Client requires an offer of finance of the contract with the bid. If so, the availability of finance will need to be reconfirmed after receipt of the invitation.

Allocate bidding tasks

Where the parties bidding together are located in different countries, separate clearly defined tasks should be allocated to each member.

Finance may also need to be secured from sources in several countries. The bidding programme should allow realistic lead times for these activities. There should be adequate provision for the parties to come together to finalize the bid.

Consistency of the whole set of documents which will form the tender elements should be planned at this time.

Bidding tactics

After initial analysis of the tender documents, it will be necessary to establish the basic tactics to be employed. This includes decisions on

● alternative designs

● alternative programmes

● alternative finance

- scope of the conditions of contract and need to qualify them: where the conditions of contract are to be proposed by the bidder, they have to be agreed between the parties as soon as possible; if possible, the parties should be asked to agree to use standard forms

- need to get legal, commercial and technical advice and assistance, on contractual matters and on operating within the country

- need for additional geotechnical information

- how much subcontracting

- agent's activities

- currency-hedging.

Site visit

Comprehensive check-lists of information required have to be prepared before the site visit, as described in chapter 2.

During the site visit

- local suppliers and subcontractors should be interviewed and enquiries issued

- communications with head offices of the partners should be established

- the scope of the agent's activities should be established.

Technical analysis prior to pricing

In parallel with the site visit, the key most substantial temporary works should be designed. Information for this should be obtained from the site visit.

The key construction activities that most affect time and money should be analysed and method statements produced. These are needed to provide the basis for estimating the cost of the works and for establishing where qualifications to the enquiry documents or adjustments to the design and scope of the works are necessary.

Method statements should establish the key rates of output and resources required for the project and determine the outline of the construction programme. Method statements should also be the main factor influencing the selection of construction equipment.

18

The selection of equipment has of course to relate to the particular problems that may be inherent in the location of the project.

Databanks

The key output and price elements of the bid must be mutually established by the partners as early as possible. Certainly on completion of the site visit and technical analysis, a common databank should be confirmed.

Conditions of contract

The conditions of contract should be examined in detail. Particular care should be taken to find out if the laws of the country modify or overrule certain conditions of contract.

Matters relating to bonds and insurances need to be identified and circulated as soon as possible to the organizations who should deal with them.

Matters which need clarifying with the issuing authorities or need a local legal opinion should be dealt with during the site visit.

Where an offer of finance has to be made, the banks or financial advisers must be sent copies of the relevant conditions of contract as soon as possible.

Funding

In some bids there will be a requirement by the Client for finance to be arranged for the project. This is likely to be on a concessionary basis rather than on unsubsidized commercial terms. Accordingly, a bank will be required as financial adviser and arranger, and negotiations should take place with export funding agencies in parallel with the preparation of the tender.

The bidding programme has to allow for the time required by these institutions, and has to provide for the stages when information has to be transferred between the bid and the loan agreement (while the latter is in preparation). A number of costs such as premiums have to be incorporated in the bid and there may also be circumstances when cross-subsidies have to be allowed for.

Because many export credit agencies require to see the completed contract, it is unlikely that the loan agreement can come into force on signature of contract, and usually loan offers are made subject to availability of funds and other circumstances. Accordingly, there will be a period after signature of the contract before it can become effective.

Where funding is made as an alternative to the finance supplied by the Client, similar circumstances prevail and time must be allowed in the programme to accommodate the arrangements.

Programming and estimating

The construction programme should be resourced with the main activities which determine the shape and competitiveness of the bid.

The principal elements of a tender in a developing country are

- labour   5–8%

- materials   15–25%

- equipment   15–35%

- subcontractors   0–45%

- site overheads
- head office   } 15–30%

There is unlikely to be an active equipment-hire market in the locality of the project. Nor is there is likely to be continuity of employment of equipment between projects. The competitiveness of a bid may therefore depend on the terms of the supply, capitalization and disposal of plant, and the cost and difficulties of providing spare parts.

The times needed to obtain equipment and materials will be critical determinants of the overall construction period. Problems in this area should be analysed and then listed in a lead-time schedule of key items.

The time required to prepare the estimate will be a function of the number and location of the parties who have to be co-ordinated. Consultations with agents and local representatives will also tend to stretch the time needed.

Adequate time must be allowed for the reconciliation of the make-up of the tender, the company's procedures for approving bids, and the collection of the required documentation, including bonds, guarantees and insurances. Where joint ventures are involved, this will normally involve exchange of parent company letters of guarantee between the partners.

The final intercompany agreements should also be signed at this time.

If funding is to be offered, the collection of the final documentation relating to this will also impose programme restraints. It is likely that these final actions, together with the time needed to deliver the documents, will require at least three weeks.

4 Negotiating a contract: post-bid submission

After submission of bids it is unlikely that a contract award will be made without a period of negotiation. This will be so even when a low bid is unqualified and finance is provided by a multilateral funding agency.

Where an offer of funding is included with the bid the negotiating of the construction contract will be iterative, with the parallel negotiation of the loan agreement. As the loan agreement will be subject to both the terms and the legality of the construction contract, it is most likely to be signed after the contract has been signed. In the case of the inclusion of concessionary export finance in the loan, the period between signature of the contract and signature of the loan agreement may be several months. Because the construction contract is likely to be subject to the provision of finance, it may not come into effect until the loan agreement is signed.

A typical schedule of conditions precedent to contract effectiveness is shown in Fig. 5 for a loan situation.

Support by local agent

During the post-bid negotiations, there will inevitably be an attempt by the Client to obtain concessions in terms and price from the low bidder. This will normally involve giving opportunities to the second or other bidders to reduce their prices.

It is in such a situation that the effectiveness of the local agent will be demonstrated. Because of the extreme bureaucracy of most developing countries, and prevailing vested interests in some, it is essential to select an agent who will properly represent the bidding company.

The circumstances of the negotiations will usually be unfair to the bidder, and it is only by having an accurate two-way flow of

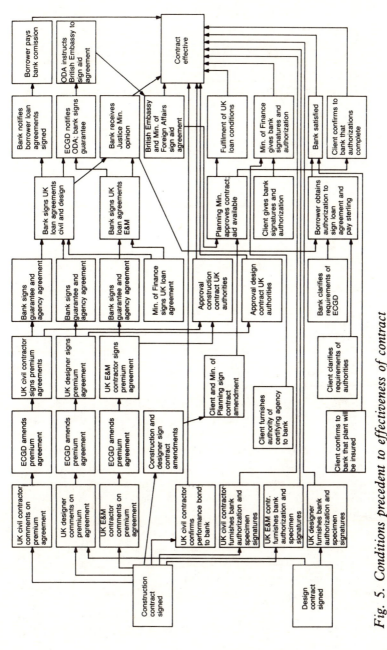

Fig. 5. Conditions precedent to effectiveness of contract

information through an agent that some balance is established.

An agent having been appointed, it is vital that his advice is taken. It is also essential that his fee is based on success.

Topics for negotiation

A number of matters may be brought up during negotiations which were not included in the invitation to bid. These may include

- the appointment of local suppliers and subcontractors
- the use of specific handling and ports-clearance agents
- the use of ships under host country flag.

Some matters which may have had to be qualified in the bid should also be clarified during this period, such as

- work permits for UK and other expatriate staff
- payment of import duties
- taxation.

Negotiation team

It is normal to have several negotiations of the various technical and commercial terms of a contract going at the same time on different aspects of a bid, with different client teams, and substantial resources may have to be committed to this activity. In some cases the Client's resources may be limited and the same people may be fielded for different subjects, thereby extending the overall time period. The Author has the experience of negotiations of a major hydro-power scheme in Indonesia where the detailed negotiations required the presence of some 30 personnel for a period of three months, and a thermal power station in China where design was also involved and over 40 people were required for up to nine months.

Personnel at the home offices will be required to support the site teams, but a high level of decision-making must be vested in the site people and they must be led by people who are seen by the Client to represent their companies. At least there must be an arrangement for approvals to be obtained on all main issues within 24 hours.

Negotiations normally take a long time. There may be many days of waiting for meetings. When they do take place they are likely to be called at a moment's notice at any time of day. It is important to keep up morale during these proceedings. Personnel must be housed where there are adequate recreational facilities. If the period is likely to be extended, sufficient staff should be involved to allow some trips home (with the excuse of the need for consultation, for example).

It is most important that there is no undue pressure to give concessions to 'get it over with'. However, some deadline should be created to stimulate the Client to reach a conclusion — such as a date when interest rates on the loan change or when some facility will no longer be available. For this to be effective, it must seem to be beyond the power of the bidder to extend the deadline.

Negotiation budget

All of the above obviously adds up to a very high rate of expenditure and it is important that a budget is prepared for this before the bid is submitted. A situation must not be allowed to develop where so much unforeseen cost has accumulated that there is a strong pressure to make concessions rather than face a write-off of the 'investment'. There must be milestones established from the time of the initial decision to bid where walkaway decisions are made if the required circumstances do not materialize.

5 Mobilizing

On award of a contract, a special team should be set up to mobilize the project. The principal tasks of this team are

- to plan the start-up activities and prepare a start-up manual
- to set up and develop a start-up organization
- to establish communication links with the Client, other companies and authorities
- to assemble all the contract documentation, including prebid agreements
- to complete the intercompany agreements
- to obtain temporary office premises in the lead company's home office and in the territory of the project
- to mobilize and brief a team to establish a presence in the territory
- to organize a programme of formal start-up meetings
- to set up a mobilization progress- and cost-monitoring system, including an action plan
- to organize the start of project planning and resource mobilization
- to induct permanent project staff and progressively hand over responsibility to them

Start-up team

The start-up team should consist of the following personnel, on a full-time or part-time basis

- operations director of company responsible for the project
- divisional or company administration manager, or equivalent
- nominated support-office manager or temporary stand-in from planning department
- company plant director
- company or divisional procurement manager
- company or divisional chief accountant
- company or divisional personnel manager

If the designated Project Manager is available he should also be a member of the team. He and the support-office manager should be the working core of the team at the early start-up stage, and to them should be added further staff as permanent or temporary members of the early start-up organization.

If a loan agreement has been undertaken the company project finance manager should also be a member of the team.

Project Manager

The title *Project Manager* is used throughout this book to denote the contractor's authorized executive and top manager appointed to take charge of the project in the territory. Various other titles may be used in practice; for instance, Project Director. What matters are the role and its responsibilities.

Start-up manual

A project-specific start-up manual should be compiled from the company's procedures for mobilizing projects. This should be started immediately by the team and should be targeted for issue within two months of commencement. The manual should contain

- reference (only) to standard procedures and manuals to be used on the project
- detailed procedures specific to the individual project or territory
- any additional information which will be helpful to the start-up teams, both in head office and on site.

After any necessary consultation with the heads of functional

27

departments, and using information collated by the support-office manager, the operations director should finalize and issue the manual. The manual should be issued to all senior staff in both the UK and site start-up teams, with copies to the heads of functional departments as appropriate.

Not all the required information will be available within the two-month period: initial issue should be made at that time, with the additional information added in later issues. The start-up manual should transmutate later into the organization and procedures manual for the project.

Typical contents for the manual are

- introduction
  o general description of the contract and its objectives
  o the relationships of the parties
  o statement of the aims and use of the manual

- administration
  o list of standard divisional and company procedures to be used on the contract
  o notes on any specific amendments to standard procedures in the above list
  o names of those to whom divisional procedures and manuals are to be issued (may be incorporated in list of standard divisional and company procedures above)
  o map of the territory showing location of site in relation to major towns, ports etc., to help UK-based staff to appreciate the distances involved
  o addresses and telephone and telex numbers of site and other relevant offices (including Client, Engineer, agents, government offices, UK embassy)
  o communications: reference numbers, filing system (UK and site), mail arrangements, mailbag frequency, document-control system, radio links
  o check-list of reports and returns required, stating if 'shuttle copies' of progress charts, etc. are wanted
  o stationery: arrangements for printing; in UK and on site; start-up supplies
  o schedule of meetings, with dates where possible: internal to company, with joint venture partners, with Client/Engineer (in UK or countries of joint venture partners, or in territory

of works), with plant department, with subcontractors/
suppliers
- o issue of contract documents and tender correspondence
- o project diary

- • expatriate staff
- o expatriate staff organization chart
- o expatriate staff bar chart, showing dates required on site
- o job descriptions
- o expatriate staff terms and conditions of service, including
  standard allowances, method of payment, local income tax and
  other tax obligations, travel arrangements, including baggage
  allowances and arrangements for shipment to site, insurance
  of personal effects
- o notes on country for expatriate staff (issued separately later);
  responsibility for preparation to be clearly stated in manual
- o accommodation arrangements: married staff, messing,
  temporary
- o welfare arrangements, including medical
- o security arrangements
- o training
- o schooling for accompanying children
- o immigration procedures

- • cash and finance
- o banking arrangements, signatories, funding
- o exchange control, if applicable
- o cash-handling, security, safes, accountability
- o financial reporting
- o funding drawdown procedure
- o pre-disbursement conditions
- o local auditors
- o taxation procedures

- • planning
- o planning methods and procedures, including materials-testing
  arrangements
- o start-up action plan and review procedure
- o document control procedure
- o temporary works design procedure

- • plant and transport

o arrangements for supply of fuels and lubricants
o fuel storage and control
o initial-spares ordering and shipment
o schedule of plant workshops and maintenance equipment required
o warranty, insurance and accident claims procedure
o tender plant schedules
o buyback arrangements
o local hire
o start-up workshop and stores

● temporary and permanent materials and subcontracts
o shipping arrangements, carriers, agents: air, sea, land
o packing requirements
o shipping documentation and marks
o customs clearance procedures and prohibited items
o marine insurance claims procedure
o storage, including local legal requirements regarding hazardous materials
o ordering approval procedures
o tender material schedules
o contract materials inspection requirements

● site start-up
o setting-out requirements
o survey, drawing office and laboratory equipment
o procurement of initial tools, equipment and huts
o signboards and signs

● safety
o local safety authority and regulations; use of company health and safety guidelines
o initial order for safety equipment: helmets etc.
o responsibility for publishing safety rules: designation of hard hat areas etc.
o accident and inspection registers
o application of company falsework procedures, if applicable

● costing — a specially prepared procedure may be desirable, particularly for cost reimbursable-contracts, or where partners in a joint venture do not wish to adopt one of their existing standard procedures — alternatively, the manual may contain

o   reference to company procedures, with note of amendments or particular points of importance
o   initial list of indirect and direct cost allocation codes — at least sufficient for the first six months of construction
o   plant cost arrangements; plant groups
o   materials cost allocation, and whether at requisition/order/issue stage

●   labour
o   engagement of labour: documentation, authority, wage scales, trade testing, medical examination etc.
o   arrangements and regulations concerning third-country nationals, if applicable
o   casual labour: documentation and pay
o   labour payroll: statutory deductions, method, frequency, advances, subsistence
o   training
o   welfare

●   insurances: reporting instructions and claims procedure in respect of contract all risks, third party, employer's liability, personal accident, workmen's compensation, marine and shipment of goods (see plant and transport, above), personal effects, in transit/on site/in territory, professional indemnity (if appropriate), fire (if applicable), non-ratification of contract, subcontractors, political risks, motor (cars and vehicles), construction works guarantee, wrongful-call insurance on bonds and guarantees, money, fidelity (if applicable), aircraft, medical

●   commercial
o   document receipt, issue and recording (part of document control procedure)
o   meetings
o   procedures on site instructions, submissions certification, payment and contractual records
o   retention money and bonds.

Development of the start-up organization
Key members
The start-up organization should commence by bringing together the various heads of the company or division functional

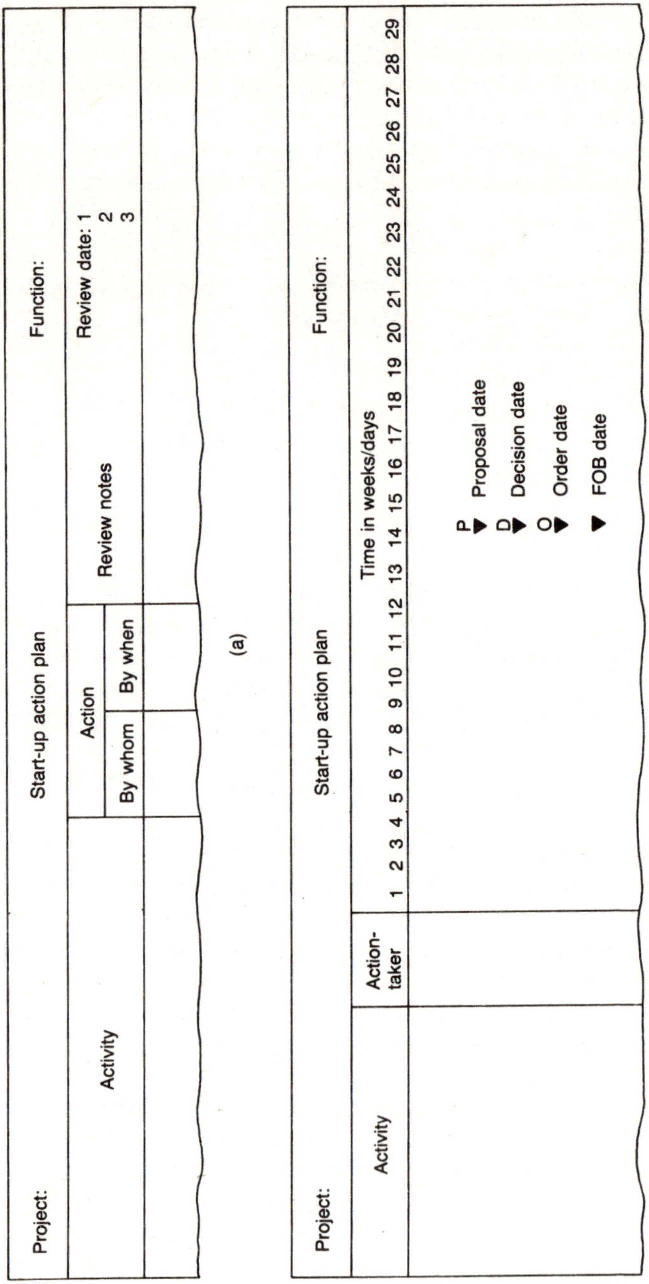

Fig. 6. Mobilization action plan

departments. This allows the mobilization of the initial input of resources to the project. If the Project Manager is available, he should be installed as soon as possible and start to build up a core working team. If he is not available, the most senior designated member of his future organisation should be appointed as temporary team leader.

The second key member of the core team is the home support office manager. A description of the function of a support office is given in chapter 6. Here all that needs to be said is that this office should be located in the lead-company home office and has the sole task of providing offshore support to the project. If the designated support-office manager is not available, a member of the company or divisional planning department who was involved in the planning of the bid should be appointed temporarily.

The third key member is someone to be sent in to the territory immediately to initiate the local effort in the mobilization of the project.

Team actions

The start-up team should initially operate through a series of meetings which should be chaired by the operations director. In the case of a joint venture, a supervisory committee should be set up, and each company should have a representative in the initial start-up team and should be at the meetings. The lead-company representative should be the operations director. The heads of the functional departments of the company or companies should initially attend these meetings.

The core team should be the secretariat for the meetings. Progressively, the core team will be expanded, and the start-up activities will be more and more under the control of the core team, with the meetings acting as a policy confirmation and approval mechanism, and the day-to-day activities proceeding in accordance with a mobilization action plan as in the example in Fig. 6.

The heads of the functional departments will be less and less directly involved as the core team takes control, and contact with their departments should become more formal and structured.

The core team should be progressively expanded during the start-up phase to include all the members of the project support office and senior members of the site organization during their induction and preplanning before they move to site.

33

34

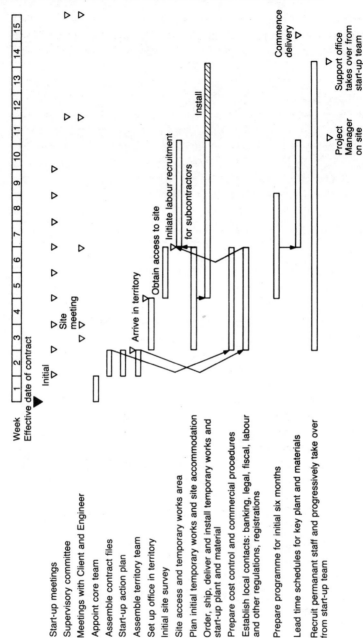

Fig. 7. Start-up programme

As soon as possible the Project Manager should take up residence in the territory of the project, and the start-up team at that stage should be led by either the next most senior member of his staff or the support-office manager.

At the beginning of the mobilization phase, the start-up team should have as temporary members the estimators and planners who were involved in the bid. Progressively, as the tender information is passed on to the project personnel, these temporary members should be redeployed.

Permanent project organization

The start-up team will gradually be superseded by the permanent project organization. A typical start-up programme is shown in Fig. 7. The activities in this programme are shown as commencing at the effective date of the contract. At the company's risk they could start on award of contract.

Contract and tender documents

The start-up team should bring together all the documentation involved in the tender. A commercial file should be prepared containing all the pre-contract correspondence and a tender make-up file should be assembled which will provide the initial input into planning, programming and cost control.

Inter-company agreements

If a joint venture is involved, the prebid agreements should be converted into full joint venture agreements in the first few weeks of the mobilization period.

If the agency agreement is not complete, it should be finalized as early as possible. Particular attention should be given to taxation implications.

If export credit is involved, a premium agreement should be signed at this stage.

The agreement with the bank organizing the funding may have to be completed in detail at this stage.

A general commercial procedure note should be prepared detailing the method of operating all agreements.

Some agreements may have to be registered in the host country, and copies of some may have to be provided in some form to the Client.

Programme of formal start-up meetings

The start-up meetings previously referred to should cover key items which have to be dealt with during the mobilization phase. Responsibility for action on each item in the following check-list should be noted, together with the date by which action is required.

- administration
  o receipt of acceptance letter and issue of notification of new work
  o initiation of contract diary
  o distribution of documents, to head office and site, including start-up manual
  o appointment of nominee for local actions
  o statutory requirements (appoint local legal representative): insurance, notices to authorities, health and welfare
  o reports and returns required
  o local purchases: policy, procedure, signatories
  o all items in start-up manual
  o bonds and insurances.

- staff
  o tasks in start-up manual
  o appointment of project manager and senior staff from existing resources
  o initiation of recruitment procedures

- cash and finance
  o tasks in start-up manual
  o finalizing of contract cash flow chart
  o arrangement of letters of credit and bills of exchange

- accommodation
  o living accommodation
  o layout of offices, stores, workshops, camp, canteen etc.
  o services: electricity, gas, telex, telephone, water, sewerage
  o equipment: office, plant and tools, survey equipment etc.
  o site working area
  o security
  o sign boards and road signs
  o welfare arrangements: canteen, club, toilets, first aid, doctor

- planning
  o preparation of start-up action plan

o preparation of programme for start-up on site
o review of tender method statement
o review tender programme; initiation of contract master programme
o agreement of principles of temporary works and formwork; schedule requirements
o submission of programme to Client; any special requirements
o construction method statement and stage programme for first six months
o submission of programmed requirements for information from Client

● document control: establishment of control system for drawings and documents in UK and on site

● plant
o scheduling of major plant requirements; decisions on purchase or hire
o schedule of tools and equipment
o fuel and lubricants
o check of activities in start-up manual

● materials
o initiation of company materials supply procedure
o preparation of key materials schedule, with lead times
o identification of materials to be obtained locally
o security and control procedures
o consideration of aggregate supplies and testing

● subcontracts
o scheduling of subcontracts
o compilation of subcontract information check-list for early subcontracts (e.g. muck-shifting)
o establishment of management procedures

● labour
o preparation of histograms of labour requirements, particularly for initial three months
o making decisions on camp and transport
o recruitment: making decisions on local or imported labour
o confirmation of policy regarding labour regulations and trades unions

- measurement and costing
- ○ meetings between project management, estimator, accountant, quantity surveyor
- ○ agreement of construction activities
- ○ preparation of schedules of cost allowances from the tender price make-up
- ○ initiation of budgetary control system and site costing system
- ○ target date for first monthly cost
- ○ arrangements with Client's representative concerning measurement and payment including dayworks

- client meetings
- ○ initial meeting with Client and his representatives
- ○ initial meeting with the Engineer's representative (if such exists) on site

- statutory and commercial arrangements to be made in territory: obtaining group recommendations for overseas contracts — statutory; commercial

- engineering
- ○ initial survey requirements
- ○ schedule and programme of information requirements
- ○ concrete mix design and testing facilities, soil testing facilities
- ○ design of temporary works

- safety
- ○ health and safety manual
- ○ obtaining local requirements prior to discussions with company safety officer
- ○ establishment of falsework procedure
- ○ ordering of safety protective equipment, appropriate to contract works

- subsequent meetings: identification of attendance at and date of subsequent meetings to monitor progress against action plan.

Site mobilization

In the mobilization of the site, the information contained in the tender site visit check-list should be consolidated and provided to the site start-up team. Any gaps in knowledge should be identified and discussed at the pre-visit briefing.

On arrival in the territory

- the team should contact the local agent, embassy, international companies operating in the territory, the client, government departments, a lawyer, auditor, clearing agents, suppliers

- facilities at the ports and airports should be examined

- the route to the site should be surveyed

- preparatory and accommodation works that can be carried out by local subcontractors should be determined

- plant items available in local market should be identified

- the availability of local transport should be reviewed

- a local legal presence should be established

- accommodation should be obtained for staff and offices in the capital city; if the site is remote from the capital, temporary accommodation should be established at site

- a bank account should be set up

- information on local medical and schooling facilities should be updated

- full list of statutory obligations should be obtained including those concerning immigration (visas, work/residential permits, labour laws), exchange control, duties and taxes

- preparation should be made for the receipt of the initial importation of plant and materials and its onward transport to site, including any road improvements and bridge-strengthening needed.

Start-up temporary works

A basic temporary works set-up will be required at site to support the commencement of operations.

Initial stores and plant maintenance facilities are essential. These should be based on standard containers which are fully weatherproofed and lined with insulating material internally protected with grease-resistant sheeting. Each container should have its own services which can be interlocked and connected to the service module. The containers should be fully fitted out with

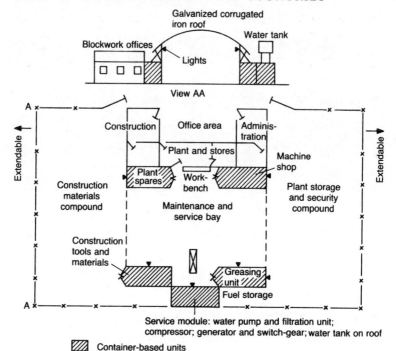

Service module: water pump and filtration unit;
compressor; generator and switch-gear; water tank on roof

▨ Container-based units

Fig. 8. Start-up temporary works and office area: overall area 25 m × 25 m, about ⅛ ha minimum

shelving and equipment appropriate to their use. One of the units should have machine shop equipment and another should have greasing and servicing equipment. All initial spares, materials and loose structural materials for the set up should be stored securely within the modules, in a way that will prevent movement during transportation.

A temporary works arrangement and minimum stores and workshop set-up is shown in Fig. 8.

All initial site documentation should be boxed and carried in one of the containers.

Site offices are best built by local means, of either timber or blockwork, depending on availability and local culture.

It is essential that this set-up can be functional within the first week of the arrival of equipment on site. After the completion of the permanent site facilities, the units can be redeployed around the site.

Meetings with Client, Engineer and Resident Engineer

An early meeting should take place in the territory with the representatives of the Client and the Engineer. Routine meetings should be established following this initial meeting. The agenda for the initial meeting should include

- introductions
- communications: correspondence, copies, addresses
- issue of contract documents
- starting date
- meetings programme
- returns, reports and records
- measurement, submissions, certification and payment procedures
- offices and accommodation
- services and supplies to Client and Engineer's representatives
- where funding is provided, drawdown procedure
- preparation of contract programme
- Client assistance on importation of goods and work permits
- legal and fiscal requirements
- notices
- local labour recruitment and use of subcontractors: political factors.

This meeting should be followed by a more detailed one on the site of the works, to cover

- initial survey of boundaries, ground levels, site photographs, occupation of the site and relationships with local land-owners
- agreement on methods of survey and setting out
- quarries and borrow pits
- agreement on concrete mix design and testing
- local labour recruitment

- ascertainment of the Resident Engineer's requirements for routine returns
- agreement on methods of site measurement
- agreement on methods of site instructions
- agreement on procedure for variation of price
- agreement on dayworks procedure
- agreement on new rates procedure, including summary of on-costs and labour costs
- agreement as to how material excavated in earthworks is classified as suitable or unsuitable for incorporation in the works.

All this should be achieved through specific meetings appropriate to the size of the project.

6 Operations

The key resources of supervisory staff, labour, plant and materials are dealt with in other chapters. This chapter deals with the co-ordination and direction of the resources, and the organizational structures involved.

Organization

The special features that shape construction organizations in the developing world are

- representation of the company or joint venture in the territory

- remoteness from home base

- length of supply line for resources.

The organization may have to be registered as a local company, but even when it is not it will have a number of legal and fiscal duties that are described later. The structure therefore will resemble a company structure rather than a contractor's site organization in the UK.

Subsidiary offices may have to be set up at airports and seaports where resources are arriving and in the capital city or other locations where the Client and authorities have offices if these are some way from the site. The main office may not be at site in all cases, and may have to be moved during the period of the contract. It may initially be located in the capital at the start-up, move to the site when a reasonable level of communications has been established, and finally move to where the Client is located for the period of settling the contract final account.

An example of an organization for constructing a large project in the developing world is shown in Fig. 9. In many ways this organization is not different from one that would be adopted for

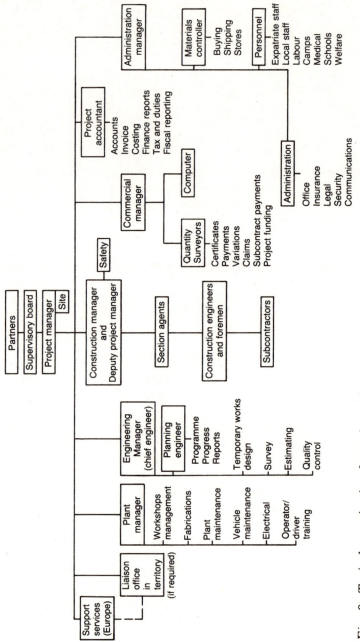

Fig. 9. Typical organization for major project

a UK-based project. The differences are due to the need to operate as a legal entity within the territory and to maintain lines of supply and communication. These features are discussed more fully later.

Supervisory board

Where a joint venture is involved, a supervisory board is needed to look after the shareholders' interests. The Project Manager should be appointed to this board and given executive responsibility by it for the execution of the contract and all the liabilities and duties of the organization in the territory.

The authority of the Project Manager should be clearly stated and minuted by the supervisory board, and relevant parts of the statement of authority should be issued as required to the Client and relevant authorities in the territory.

The board should be responsible for the policy of the joint venture and for the security of its investments and associated assets, including final liquidation of these. The provision of funds and the distribution of surpluses are the responsibility of the board.

The supervisory board may best operate through a series of meetings at regular intervals in the territory of the project, preferably at site. At these meetings the Project Manager should provide a report covering

- progress
- operating performance and end forecasts
- personnel, including health and safety
- Client relations
- security
- in-territory relationships: legal, fiscal and public
- contractual matters
- resource deficiencies.

A typical agenda for a supervisory board meeting has the following items

- minutes of previous meeting
- matters arising

Record of site visit by		Contract Date		Date of last 'Record' Number completed this year Week number	
Key area	Review of current situation	Yes	No	Comment	
Achievement of physical progress targets	1 Have objectives agreed on last visit been initiated/achieved? 2 Are all programmes marked up to date? 3 Is progress in relation to overall programme as planned? 4 If not, time gained/lost with reasons for variance – this period? – cumulative? 5 Do current stage programmes exist for all sections and do they tie in with overall programme milestone dates? 6 Is progress in relation to stage programmes as planned? 7 Do weekly work schedules exist for all key resources and do they tie in with the stage programmes? 8 Are they being used to plan and control daily progress effectively?				
Tour of site	9 Are critical activities in accordance with weekly work schedule? 10 Are site and temporary works laid out as planned and working effectively? 11 Are materials being stored and protected correctly? 12 Is quality of work to specification? 13 Is site safety up to statutory regulations? 14 Is site welfare maintained to Company standards? 15 Is morale of key management personnel satisfactory? 16 Is level of labour and plant activity satisfactory? 17 Is the level of site setting-out errors acceptable?			Scaffolding............ Excavation............ Housekeeping............ Access .... Report checked	
Achievement of financial targets	18 Have costs of labour and plant been contained within allowance? 19 Have GEs been contained within allowance? 20 Is the cumulative actual allowance earned up to budget? 21 Is the cumulative actual cost contained within budget? 22 Is the cumulative contribution to overhead and profit up to budget? 23 Have contract variations, delays and claims been correctly dealt with? 24 Is the QS monthly measure up to date and accurate?				
Materials purchasing, planning and control	25 Are key materials being ordered and delivered according to schedule? 26 Have supply difficulties been checked out? 27 Are key material losses acceptable – on price in relation to estimate? – on reconciliation?				

Fig. 10

- review of progress by each section manager

- costs, budgets and forecasts

- review of resources: staff, labour (including recruitment and travel), plant (including shipping), materials (including shipping)

- review of programmes

- planning activities

- contractual matters

- funding and payment

- security, accidents and insurance claims

- public relations

- other business

- action list arising from meeting

- date of next meeting.

The supervisory board visit should consists of at least two days at site and one day in the town where the Client is located. A visit to the Client and the Engineer should be included in every itinerary.

The site visit should allocate one day for a detailed examination of the site and one day for the board meeting. This should also allow a social evening to be spent with the staff and their spouses.

The site visit should be conducted on a formal basis. As a discipline, each member of the supervisory board should compile a record of the type illustrated in Fig. 10. A copy of each of these should be included in the information left with the Project Manager at the end of the visit. This information pack should also include the action list from the meeting.

Where the works are carried out by a single contractor and not by a joint venture, the site visit procedure should be carried out with equal formality and structure by the operations director and any home office staff accompanying him.

Services

Many services need to be provided to an overseas project, both in the territory and at the home base.

Where a joint venture is involved, one of the members should act as the leader. The duties should principally consist of keeping the joint venture's accounts, organizing meetings and keeping minutes, overlooking the home base support office, liaising with funding agencies, and acting as the link between the Project Manager and the supervisory board. The other members should pay a small fee for this service.

The leader should not be responsible for providing information to the joint venture shareholders from the project organization. This duty should be carried out by the home base project support office as a cost against the project, and not included in the sponsor's fee.

Because of the remoteness of the site from the home base and the need to acquire resources from there, an office is usually set up in the leader's headquarters to provide the services required. This office is a detached part of the project organization and should be under the control of the Project Manager. It is usual for the project leader also to supervise these activities on behalf of the Project Manager.

Where funding requires substantial supplies of resources from particular countries, more than one support facility may have to be set up. Bilateral funding from the home countries of each of the joint venture partners may require that each partner sets up a support office. Co-ordination of these could be by one of the offices concerned or by the site office.

If funding comes from countries other than those of the joint venture partners, arrangements may be necessary to have purchasing agents in these countries. Co-ordination of these should preferably be by the site, if communications will allow.

In general, all such offices should be considered as detached parts of the Project Manager's organization.

Role of support office
In general, the role of a home-based project support office is

- provision of home-based information
- drawings and design information
- correspondence from joint venture partners and agent
- company procedures
- instructions from supervisory board

o transfer of documents: bills of lading etc.
o minutes of supervisory board and other meetings

● provision of information to joint venture partners from project site office
o cost and progress reports
o requests for and notices of release of staff
o financial information
o information on acquisition of assets
o programmes and planning information

● carrying out tasks on behalf of project organization
o processing insurance and warranty claims
o making purchases and progressing deliveries
o arranging shipping and air freight
o arranging staff travel
o making returns and carrying out actions required by funding authorities
o transferring funds
o making contacts with home-based specialists and with the Engineer's home office

● maintaining a duplicate set of all project records and correspondence

● operating a mail-bag and courier service.

Local liaison office

It may also be necessary to maintain separate offices in the territory of the project. During the central period of the contract, the main project office is normally at the site of the works. This may be remote from the airport or seaport of entry into the country and from the Client's head office, and further liaison offices may need to be set up in these locations. Local purchases may also need to be organized through these offices.

Day-to-day contacts with the agent or local sponsor should also be through these offices.

Progressing of documents through the Client's and government offices should either be carried out by the liaison office or by the agent. If it is done by the agent it should be co-ordinated by the liaison office.

External services will have to be provided locally, and these should normally be co-ordinated by the liaison offices. They include

- legal representation
- auditors
- medical services
- port and airport clearing agents
- inland transport
- radio and telephone services
- banking and exchange controls
- immigration and work permits
- labour regulations
- local insurances and claims
- vehicle and other licences
- computer services
- shipping-out arrangements
- air travel.

Contact with the embassies of the joint venture partners should be through the liaison office.

Relationships

The structure of the project organization will resemble that of a company during the continuity of the contract.

There will be requirements to establish relationships with a number of authorities, as shown in simplified form for a bilaterally funded project in Fig. 11. This requires the employment of staff who are not directly involved in the construction of the works but who carry out the duties normally undertaken by a company head office.

The Client will expect the operation of the contract to take place in the territory, and the appropriate level of relationship has to be maintained in this regard. The Project Manager will be expected to speak for the companies and to commit them. An independent Engineer may be appointed by the Client. It is more likely that this role is shared between a consultant organization and members of the Client's own staff, and that an employee of the Client is designated the Engineer.

The consultant is likely to have a supervisory role, and to act as a certifying agent where bilateral funding is involved. This may

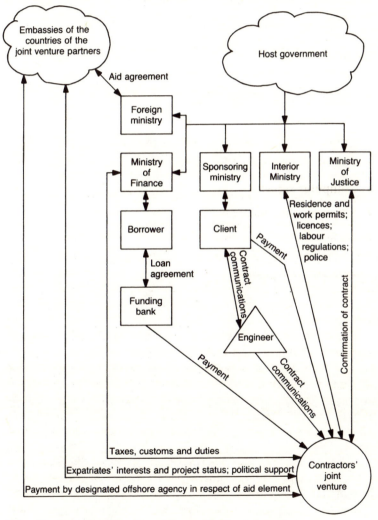

Fig. 11. Relationships in a bilaterally funded project

51

also be the role required by a multilateral agency such as the World Bank.

Living in a foreign country places a burden on the organization beyond that carried by a company within its home territory. Expatriate behaviour outside working hours and off the work site becomes the responsibility of the project organization. This and the associated staff security aspects are dealt with in chapters 7 and 11.

Communications

Communications are considered in two aspects

- structure and systems

- transfer of information.

In the past 5−10 years the communication facilities available have changed radically, even within relatively primitive countries. In particular, satellite links have reduced dependence on local networks and international connections. These links are expensive and their use is subject to the agreement of the authorities within the host countries, and so should only be used if the local telecommunications system is inadequate.

For the outlay of around £1 million, an independent communications structure can be established at the beginning of a major project, for voice and facsimile reproduction traffic. Subject to security considerations, this can also be used to connect computer systems.

Establishment of the main office at site will be dependent on securing communication linkages. Before a telephone system is connected, a radio link may be obtained subject to the permission of the authorities. Where there are no specific military considerations involved in the zone of operations, this permission is usually forthcoming. The radio link should also be maintained after telephone connections have been established, as a useful back-up system.

A code book should be introduced as early as possible to provide for secure voice transmissions. Using scramblers should also be considered.

A mail-bag service on a weekly basis between the home-based support office and either the project main office or the liaison office in the territory should be established at the time of setting up in the local base.

Routine information to be transferred between the home-based support office and the project main office should include

- monthly progress reports

- monthly operating statements and end forecasts

- staff movements

- shipment status reports

- cash movements and statements

- funding drawdown reviews and forecasts of sufficiency of funds

- report on status of the contract.

Routine information passing between the Client, the Engineer and the contractor should be as required by the contract, but is likely to include

- progress reports

- payment forecasts and actual receipts

- contractual matters.

Communications should also be established through a programme of routine site meetings with the Client and supervising engineer.

Non-routine communications between the project main office and the home-based support office should cover the items referred to in the subsection in this chapter on the role of the support office.

A documentary control system should be adopted as early as possible. The system should be computerized if possible and should coded to identify

- storage location

- originator

- activity

- sub-activity

- sequence

- destination.

There should be duplication of documents, both in the home-based support office and in the main project office. Retrieval should be equally easy in the two offices.

Legal and fiscal duties

When operating in a foreign country, it may be necessary by law either to form a local company or to register a branch. This will place additional reporting obligations on the local organization. Some of the following obligations will be incurred even where neither a local company nor a branch is involved

- registration to be an employer and to contract for supplies and services

- registration to carry out the type of work required by the contract

- filing such company or branch returns as are required by law

- making tax returns and getting tax clearance

- complying with labour laws

- obtaining work permits for expatriates and making associated returns

- ensuring that expatriates comply with tax regulations

- complying with the regulations on transfer of money

- obtaining licences for vehicles, communications etc.

- complying with regulations for customs clearance, and payment or relief of duties

- obtaining and maintaining insurances and bonds.

The full range of specific obligations should be established as early as possible. Many should have been identified during the prebid site visit, but should be rechecked for possible changes of regulations.

7 Staff

On an overseas project, the staff resource is the one which determines the competitive ability of companies. Assets such as construction plant are purchased on the international market and usually, in the case of large projects, sold at the end of contracts. Labour is substantially, if not entirely, local, and in countries such as in the Middle East where labour has to be imported, it is usually obtained from developing countries.

The quality and care of staff is the difference between successful and unsuccessful companies. The maintenance of this quality and the creation of an effective working environment in often difficult conditions is the prime task of management. In the home base, involvement of the employing company with its staff is usually confined to the work site and the time spent there. Overseas, and particularly in a developing country, this involvement spans not only the whole of the period in the territory but also all the accompanying dependants of the employed person. The Project Manager on an overseas project must be an effective leader of his community.

The provision, maintenance and effective use of the staff resource involves

- resource plan
- selection
- transference
- accommodation and support
- discipline and reimbursement
- return to base.

Resource plan

In preparing the staff resource plan, the following should be considered

- *capability and level of skill of anticipated labour force:* this determines the proportions of staff to labour

- *availability of local staff of sufficient skill:* tribal considerations may be involved; it may not be possible in the specific location to use the tribe with the adequate skill level, and therefore expatriates may have to be used

- *technology and skill transfer:* the resource plan may require expatriates to be introduced at the early stages in jobs that can be filled later by locals after they have received sufficient training; this requires the expatriates to be chosen for their training and communication abilities

- *quota restrictions:* these may limit staff recruitment from certain countries

- *resource levelling:* if, when constraints on supply are examined, it appears necessary to alter the work programme because of deficiencies, this must be done and the consequences accepted; because of scarce expatriate management resources, the ability to supervise night-shift working may be questioned; alternatively, it may be that the work can be organized so that the activities on the critical path can be more highly supervised than others

- *accompanied and unaccompanied staff:* the relative proportions of these must be established with care; while it is more expensive to accommodate dependants, it provides a more stable community; in some cases it may be the only way that some levels of staff will accept employment, particularly if the home base is offering good employment prospects; the ability to provide secure accommodation for dependants is an important factor for consideration; alternatively, unaccompanied staff may have to be provided with very generous leave and travel entitlements; apart from the cost, this will result in a larger staff resource to cover for people on leave, as a result the pure price comparison may not be so biased in favour of unaccompanied staff.

Selection

Principally, this section relates to the selection of expatriate staff. The selection of local staff is dealt with in the section on labour.

Third-country recruitment

Recruiting staff from a third country is usually done for three reasons

- language

- special skills

- cheapness.

Obviously, there are particular problems in third-country recruitment unless the company has established operations or offices in that country. Alternatively, there may be individuals who have worked for the company in other territories and have established reputations with the company.

If possible, new staff who are to fill key roles should pass through a training and indoctrination period. If possible, it should be at the home base; if not, these members of staff should start in a closely supervised role.

If cheapness is the motive for recruitment, staff are unlikely to be transferred on an accompanied basis, as the overall cost difference in such cases is unlikely to be enough to warrant selection from a third-country source.

Home-base recruitment

In selecting expatriate staff from the home base, the following qualities must be examined

- appropriate skill

- leadership

- emotional stability

- compatibility with local culture

- medical fitness.

Skill is an obvious aspect which should be examined in any job selection situation, whether at home or overseas. The others are either peculiar to or of greater importance in a foreign environment.

In a home-based situation, lack of real leadership qualities can often be disguised and compensated for by particular job based knowledge and ability, and as the relationships cultivated need only be site-based and for working hours, strains may not show. For this reason, candidates without overseas working experience recorded by the company must be interviewed and tested just as intensively as newcomers. At home promotion may not be based on character. Overseas, this is a vital ingredient in success.

Similarly, staff transferred to Third World locations often suffer culture shock, so it is necessary to determine whether or not they have sufficient emotional stability to adjust successfully.

There is also an equal need to be able to live, day in and day out, within a closed expatriate community. Some individuality which can be tolerated or even admired at home may not be appropriate in a community overseas.

Local culture

It is important that expatriate staff give due consideration to local culture, both in their relationships with the labour force they supervise and in the contacts they make outside work. Local sensitivity must be recognized and accommodated. This applies to dress, speech and manner. Religious and tribal aspects of local culture should be understood. Before staff are transferred to new territories, information and lectures on local culture should be organized, and attended both by the staff and their accompanying dependants.

This latter involvement is important. Interviews for suitability should include both the staff and their spouses. The disruption to a closed expatriate community by family conflict or inability to conform or compromise on the part of the spouse can be devastating. The psychological make up of the partners and the perceived stability of the marriage are key issues that must be evaluated. How a wife will relate to a situation where she has no outside job and, because of the availability of servants, has excess time on her hands must be carefully assessed.

Interviews of this nature should take place in a relaxed and social atmosphere. They should include at least one session over a meal in a restaurant.

All staff and their accompanying dependants must be subject to a successful medical examination before transfer overseas. A controlled psychological test must be included in the recruitment procedure.

Selection criteria
   The overall selection procedure should include a formal report on

- knowledge of relevant work
- previous overseas experience
- management skills
- reaction to the unexpected (a psychological test should be set up)
- leadership qualities
- sympathy and understanding (another psychological test)
- drive and energy
- leisure activities (whether sole, or team-based)
- domestic situation
- health (signs of stress, hidden problems etc. as well as physical well-being)
- personal appearance and demonstration of confidence.

Transfer

   Before staff are transferred into a territory, entry, residence and work permits are needed. In most cases the names and details of the persons involved are required for the applications. It is therefore possible that weeks or months may pass before a person selected can be transferred to the territory. This period should be used in indoctrination, training and testing. This programme should also involve the spouse where appropriate. Tasks associated with the project that can be carried out from the home base should also be included.

   The member of staff, if possible, should proceed to the territory in advance of his accompanying dependants. A period of some three months in advance is desirable. This should be mandatory for anyone taking up a job overseas for the first time with the company.

   All necessary inoculations should be carried out.

Travel documents and information

The travel documents for the member of staff should include

- passport, valid for at least the duration of the contract of employment

- tickets (these should include an open return, which should be handed over to the liaison office on arrival in the territory; if currency or purchase price considerations dictate otherwise, a return may not be provided)

- necessary visas and permits

- inoculation certificates

- travellers cheques for emergencies and for covering period until funds can be made available in the territory

- accommodation address in country

- advice on airport clearing procedures

- arrangements for being met at airport

- accompanying-luggage regulations and excess-allowance provision, if necessary

- insurance covering accident and baggage; this should be valid for at least for two weeks after arrival in the territory, to allow time for other arrangements to be made, either by the company or by the member of staff

- stop-over arrangements, if necessary.

When the dependants travel to meet the member of staff, similar information is provided. In addition, assistance should be provided at the departure airport.

All procedures involving class of travel, baggage allowance, insurance etc. must be made clear at the time of interview.

During the period between the member of staff arriving in the territory and the departure of the dependants, the company's personnel department must keep in touch on a regular basis with the dependants and keep them advised of the programme. Any problems that are encountered by the dependants due to the absence of the member of staff must be dealt with or advised on sympathetically by the personnel department.

In the case of the staff member being transferred on an unaccompanied basis, this procedure should continue during his period overseas.

Accommodation and support

In all foreign locations, senior management attention to the total welfare of staff is needed, much more than mere day-to-day working contacts as in the UK. Otherwise, local social or family problems can become obsessions.

Expatriate staff require a high quality of accommodation and support to make them effective in a developing country environment. This support consists of

- accommodation
- leisure activities and entertainment
- transport
- leave and travel
- schooling of children
- medical facilities.

Accommodation

The standard of accommodation should be good. This should not impose a high cost on the project. Fig. 12 shows a typical camp layout, Fig. 13 a typical detached expatriate house and Fig. 14 a semi-detached layout. Table 3 shows typical inventories of the equipment that should be provided in two- and three-bedroom houses. The construction should be in readily available local materials, either timber or blockwork. In certain countries, such as in the Middle East, it may be necessary to import prefabricated buildings.

Single quarters with good messing facilities should be provided. As well as communal rooms, single accommodation should provide sitting room facilities for the occasions when individuals wish to be on their own. An ideal layout consists of two bedrooms with a shared sitting room. There must also be a common room available to all single staff which is not shared by married families. Single staff should be provided with a separate dining room with a very good standard of food to suit national tastes.

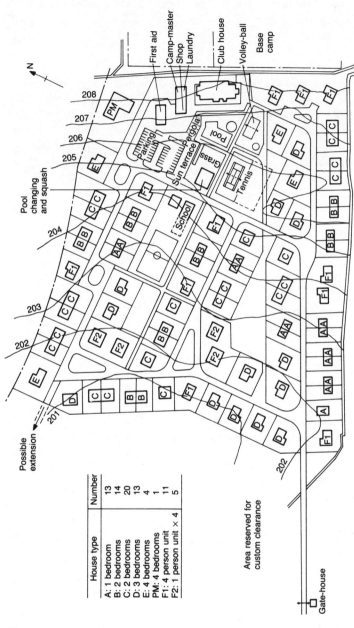

Fig. 12. Typical camp layout

House type	Number
A: 1 bedroom	13
B: 2 bedrooms	14
C: 2 bedrooms	20
D: 3 bedrooms	13
E: 4 bedrooms	4
PM: 4 bedrooms	1
F1: 4 person unit	11
F2: 1 person unit × 4	5

62

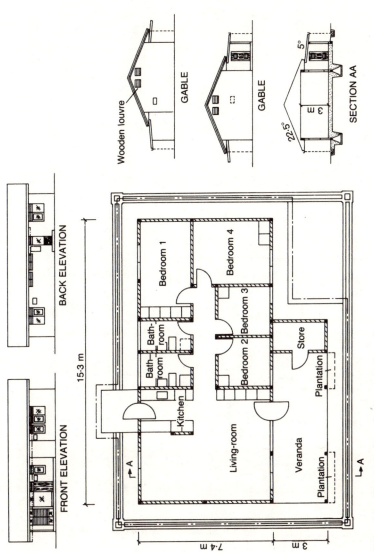

Fig. 13. Typical detached expatriate house

63

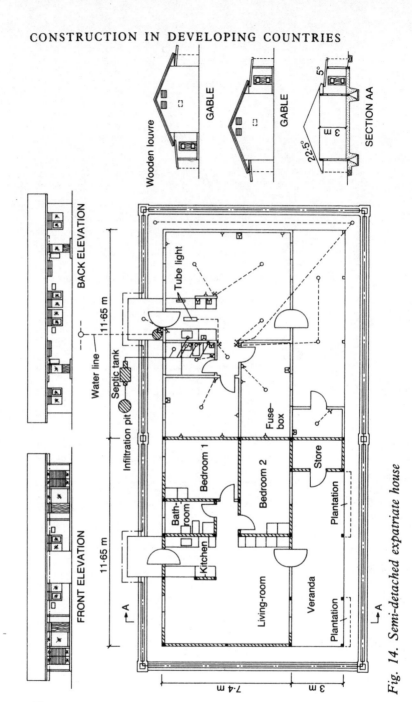

Fig. 14. Semi-detached expatriate house

Table 3. Typical inventories for two-bedroom (2B) and three-bedroom (3B) houses in a warm climate

Item	3B	2B	Item	3B	2B
Master bedroom			Chest of drawers		
Double divan bed	1	1	3-drawer	1	—
Dressing table	1	1	Single sheets	4	—
Dressing table stool	1	1	Pillow cases	4	—
Chest of drawers			Feather pillows	2	—
5-drawer	1	1	Single blankets	3	—
Bedside chest			Cot	1	—
3-drawer	2	2	Cot sheets	2	2
Bedside rug	1	1	Cot blanket	1	1
Mirror 51 in by 16 in	1	1			
Chair wooden arms	1	1	*Bathroom 1*		
Coat hangers	36	36	Bathroom cabinets	2	2
Double sheets	4	4	Bath mats towelling	4	2
Pillow cases	8	8	Shower curtains	2	1
Feather pillows	4	4	Towel rails	4	3
Double blankets	2	2	Toilet-roll holders	2	2
			Glass shelves	3	2
Bedroom 1			Bath mats rubber	2	1
Divan bed single	2	2	Bath towels	10	8
Bedside chest			Hand towels	10	8
3-drawer	2	2	Guest towels	6	6
Chair wooden arms	1	1			
Bedside rugs	1	1	*Lounge*		
Mirrors	1	—	3-piece suite	1	1
Chest of drawers			Easy chair	2	2
3-drawer	1	1	Coffee table, long	1	1
Single sheets	8	8	Coffee table, small	3	3
Pillow cases	8	8	Writing table	1	1
Feather pillows	4	4	Pair wall units	1	1
Single blankets	4	4	Standard lamp	1	1
			Table lamp	1	1
Bedroom 2			Lampshades		
Divan bed	1	—			
Bedside chest			*Dining room*		
3-drawer	1	—	Dining table	1	1
Chair wooden arms	1	—	Dining chair	8	8
Bedside rug	1	—	Sideboard	1	1
Mirrors	1	—	Side table	1	1

continued overleaf

Table 3 — continued

Item	3B	2B	Item	3B	2B
Kitchen and hardware			Squeegee floor mop	1	1
Kitchen table	1	1	Floor mop	1	1
Polypropylene chairs	4	2	Carpet sweeper	1	1
Cooker gas/electric	1	1	Colander	1	1
Refrigerator	1	1	Strainers (1 large,		
Washing machine	1	1	1 tea medium)	2	2
Pyrex dishes			Wooden spoons		
(1 medium,			(1 large, 1 medium,		
1 small)	2	2	1 small)	3	3
Casserole dishes			Kitchen forks		
(1 large, 1 small)	2	2	(1 large, 1 small)	2	2
Saucepans (1 large, 1			Kitchen knives		
medium, 1 small)	3	3	(1 large, 1 small)	2	2
Mixing bowls (1			Chopping board	1	1
large, 1 medium			Cheese board and		
Pyrex)	2	2	knife	1	1
Frying pans (1 large,			Bread board	1	1
1 medium)	2	2	Bread knife	1	1
Baking tins (cake) set			Egg beater	1	1
of 3	3	3	Cheese grater	1	1
Sponge tin	1	1	Potato peeler	1	1
Cake tin (12 cup)	1	1	Butter knife	1	1
Roasting pans			Jam dish	1	1
(1 large,			Egg cups	6	6
1 medium)	2	2	Carving set	1	1
Can opener (wall			Laundry basket	1	1
type)	1	1	Lemon squeezer	1	1
Corkscrew	1	1	Toast rack	1	1
Bottle opener	1	1	Pair teak salad		
Tea towels	6	6	servers	1	1
Dusters	6	6	Serving trays	2	2
Floor cloths	2	2	Electric toaster	1	1
Plastic buckets	2	2	Electric kettle	1	1
Dustpan and brush	1	1	Electric iron	1	1
Sweeping brushes			Ironing board	1	1
(1 hard, 1 soft)	2	2	Rotary clothes line	1	1
Scrubbing brushes	1	1	Litter bin		
Lavatory brushes and			(foot-operated)	1	1
holders	2	2	Dustbin and lid	1	1

continued on facing page

Table 3 — continued

Item	3B	2B	Item	3B	2B
Door mats	2	2	Piece tea set	8	8
Vegetable rack	1	1	Stainless steel teapot	1	1
Plate rack	1	1	Stainless steel milk		
Set kitchen scales	1	1	jug	1	1
Plastic washing-up			Stainless steel sugar		
bowl	1	1	bowl	1	1
Rolling pin	1	1	Sherry glasses	8	8
Water jug	1	1	Tumblers	8	8
Wooden clothes pegs	50	50	Half-pint glasses	8	8
Cruet sets	2	2	Waste-paper baskets	2	2
Bread bin	1	1	Set table mats	1	1
Butter dish	1	1	8 place cutlery set	1	1
Plastic self-adhesive			Set containers (for		
hooks	6	6	sugar etc.)	1	1
Ash trays (glass)	6	6	Jam spoon	1	1
Sets table cloth and			Mincer (hand)	1	1
napkins	2	2	Wall towel holder	1	1
Piece dinner set	8	8	Set of house curtains	1	1
Piece coffee set	8	8			

Leisure facilities

Leisure facilities should not be underrated. Although the staff should be encouraged to make their own entertainment as far as possible, basic facilities should be provided. These should include

- clubhouse with bar (if permitted by local law), restaurant and meeting room (cinema)

- swimming pool

- squash court and/or badminton court and/or tennis court.

The restaurant should be separate from the single-staff dining room and should provide an 'eating out' ambience.

On two projects known to the Author three-hole golf courses were provided. If land is available, such a facility is not unduly difficult to provide. Where the project is located in a city with adequate leisure facilities available, provision to the above scale will not be necessary.

Although the club facilities are provided by the company, the staff should be involved in the running of them. The constitution of the club should be properly drafted and should include

- object
- definitions
- provision and maintenance of facilities
- membership
- categories
- subscriptions
- structure
- activity committees
- management
- bar rules
- visitors
- conduct
- financial structure
- audit arrangements
- general meetings
- extraordinary general meetings
- quorum
- changes in constitution.

If the membership is from several companies and nationalities, it is important to avoid any form of discrimination.

Transport

If the project is located in a country where it is not possible or economic for expatriates to purchase their own vehicles, leisure transport should be provided. It is advisable that this is administered by the club management committee and forms part of the recreational facilities organized by it.

If the location of the project site is remote and does not provide any opportunities for local-interest leisure activities, short-duration leave periods should be provided in the nearest available centre. Whether this is at the company's or the individual's expense depends entirely on the policy of the contract. Transport should be provided to access with public transport, and the project administration office should make the necessary bookings.

Leave

Leave taken at the home base should be subject to the rules of the company or the joint venture. It is essential that these arrangements are common to all staff in a joint venture and that there are no perceived preferments.

The only differences will be between staff members who are single or unaccompanied and those who are accompanied. Home leave periods for unaccompanied staff are likely to be at intervals of at most six months, and intervals of at least twelve months should be maintained for accompanied staff.

Schooling

The schooling of accompanying children presents a particular set of problems

- mixed-age classes

- possibly mixed nationalities

- working to national curricula for entry to further education at home.

It is unlikely that a company school can provide adequate education for children beyond eleven years of age. If there are no facilities in the territory for this, recourse to boarding schools at home is inevitable. Most companies have a policy of assistance with school fees and payment for three trips per year to the territory for the children.

This system is easier for British children than for those of other nationalities due to the availability of British boarding schools. Some nationalities, such as the Dutch, send their children to British boarding schools in these circumstances.

The provision of primary education within some countries can face restrictions. These are more likely if the location is within a major urban centre. In Nigeria, for instance, British companies were not allowed to run private schools in English language in Lagos, as it was maintained that this discriminated against the locals who were also educated in English. German and French schools suffered no similar restrictions. In such circumstances, where a multinational joint venture is concerned, making the principal language other than English may avoid the difficulty.

On the teaching staff there must be at least one fully qualified teacher, so that the curricula can be carried through to the satisfaction of the education authorities when the child re-joins the home education system. If there is only a small number of pupils, say less than ten, one teacher, with the assistance of parent helpers to supervise certain activities, can cope with a mixed age class. Advice on curricula should be given by the education authorities of the countries concerned.

Given a school that is well set up and well run experience has shown that the individual attention provided to the child normally results in ready acceptance by the home education system on return.

With parental help it is usually easy to organize a broad range of activities using the available camp leisure facilities.

Constitution of school. The school should be set up with a board of governors representing the company and the parents. A typical constitution of a primary school will cover

- name

- founding companies

- object

- finance
o initial costs met by company loan
o fees paid by parents
o any company subsidy

- board of governors
o each company one member
o parent members
o between four and twelve members
o chairman, vice chairman, secretary and treasurer appointed by board
o board determines head teacher's authority

o determines school policy, recruitment and remuneration of staff
o monitors education standard

● head teacher
o responsible to board of governors
o maintains discipline
o administers, sets and maintains education standards

● final disposal of assets

● amendments to constitution

● coming into effect.

Medical facilities

The provision of medical facilities on a project can only be determined after a comprehensive survey of the whole system for dealing with medical problems. The survey should include

● air evacuation to a home-based hospital or an adequate international centre (e.g. Singapore in south-east Asia); this includes total journey time for road transport and air ambulance

● local hospital services, say within a road journey time of four hours

● emergency accident treatment, including urgent operations to stabilize patient condition after an accident, prior to transport to a medical centre

● general practitioner type facilities, including family health care.

The facilities should include at least two beds for emergencies; an ambulance, which should probably be based on the work site; and first aid and health-screening equipment. A typical clinic layout is shown in Fig. 15. Advice on equipment should be obtained from the appointed doctor if there is one, or from the local medical practitioner, who should be appointed on a consultant basis. Equipment is only needed to deal with simple operations or with stabilizing measures until the patient can be sent to a local hospital or evacuated by air.

A manual should be provided at the beginning of a contract which fully details the sequence of dealing with medical emergencies. Arrangements should be made with local hospitals and with an

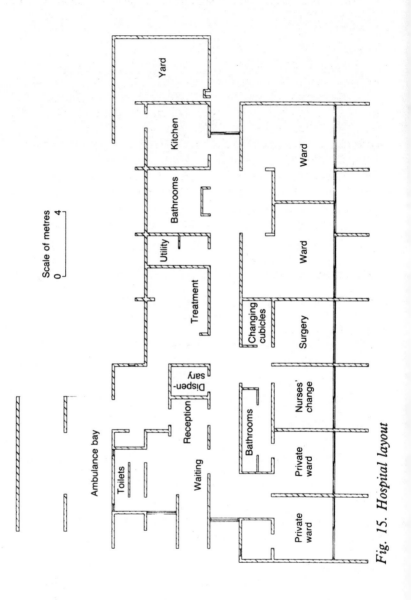

Fig. 15. Hospital layout

air evacuation facility, such as the Swiss Air Services. A qualified doctor, nurse or paramedic should be employed, depending on the size of the project.

Discipline and reimbursement

The maintenance of discipline has a higher profile in an overseas location than at home, as it involves behaviour off site as well as on.

The discipline on the job rests with the Project Manager. He is the joint venture or company's senior representative in the territory on all matters. The burden of the implementation of community discipline should be delegated to another member of his staff. This allows the Project Manager to act as a court of appeal, frees him of the continuous burden of on-site and off-site discipline, and, in fact, makes it easier for him properly to apply the on-site disciplinary procedure.

Typical candidates for the community disciplinarian would be

- project administrator
- personnel manager
- camp manager.

Discipline committee

In matters of community discipline there should be a committee of staff members to advise the discipline manager on all serious issues. This committee should establish the basic rules. These rules need to address

- relationships with locals
- behaviour and standards of dress around the camp and while using the facilities
- procedure when problems arise with local authorities.

The discipline committee should also be available to camp residents when problems arise with local authorities. In this regard it should advise and represent the party involved.

Reimbursement

Reimbursement to the expatriate is solely a matter between the individual and the employing company and as such should be dealt with either by the Project Manager or staff specifically delegated by him.

The terms of employment should be determined by the company or the joint venture. Where a multinational joint venture is involved, it is quite possible that there are different levels of remuneration for the same job if the work is carried out by different nationalities. If so, it is essential that the remuneration package is made up of separate elements of basic home-based salary and overseas uplift and incentives.

The basic home salary should be clearly seen to be typical for the job and the country concerned, and may differ widely from nationality to nationality. The overseas uplift should be the same for all job categories, irrespective of nationality. Perks and incentive payments should also be the same. This includes

- leave entitlement
- standard of accommodation
- local salary enhancement
- performance bonus.

Arrangements for making payments should depend on both local and home-based taxation systems. In some countries it may be necessary to reduce local payment to the minimum required to cover local expenses and to make all other payments offshore. In others, such as in the Middle East, one nationality may want all payments to be made locally whereas another may want to be paid through a third country which has a minimal taxation rather than no taxation (this latter used to be a requirement for Dutch staff in tax free locations).

Return to base

Expatriate staff should all be returned to their country of recruitment.

The demobilization plan should provide for accompanying dependants to be returned earlier than the employees. The aim should be that at least three months before project shutdown all dependants will have returned home. This can be related to school terms at home.

Married staff, if possible, should be released earlier than single staff. There is likely to be a natural sequence whereby commercial staff finalizing the accounts will be the last to leave. It is also likely that they will transfer from the site to the location of the Client's headquarters for a period prior to departure.

Accommodation may be handed over to the Client, sold to local parties or dismantled and removed.

Staff completing their service should be subject to tax clearance procedures. These should be prepared for well in advance. Export of belongings and import into the home country will require compliance with customs procedures, including levies.

Advice on staff return should be given in sufficient time to allow their employing companies time to arrange for redeployment or termination.

There may be goods such as motor vehicles to be disposed of in the territory.

If staff may be required to make short-duration returns during the maintenance period, it is advisable on release of residence and works permits to ensure that this can occur freely and is not subject to a time embargo.

8 Labour

A number of assumptions will have been made in the tender on the likely make-up of the labour force. Reconsideration of these is one of the key activities in the mobilization period, as previously stated. From the information obtained, a labour resource plan should be prepared.

Resource plan
The resource plan covers the following.

Sources of labour

- Can labour be imported?

- If so, from which countries can it be obtained?

- If importation is restricted or in any way undesirable, where are the sources within the country?

- Can labour be transferred economically from other parts of the country to the site?

- Would this transfer be acceptable to the local population?

- Can labour transferred from elsewhere in the country be accommodated within the local population without assistance?

Levels of skill and productivity
Labour from different Third World countries often displays different levels of skill. For instance, Sikhs tend to be good carpenters, Pakistanis good plant operators, and Filipinos good electricians. These are obviously generalizations, but tend to reflect the experience that people can gain in their own countries, and therefore a careful survey of sources is required in order to fit needs.

Within countries, particularly where there are tribal differences, different levels of skill are displayed by different peoples.

For language and general compatibility, gangs may best be made up of people of the same nationality or tribe.

The productivity of Muslims working in a Muslim country will be affected by the period of Ramadan. In such circumstances, having part of the labour force non-Muslim may increase productivity during this period.

Extent of mechanization

The type of work and in particular to what extent it will be mechanized will affect the choice of labour. Basic skill in operating earthmoving equipment can often come quite readily to people with little formal training or experience, but employing such people may require much more maintenance of the plant and possibly a larger number of expatriate maintenance staff.

The cost and availability of labour may reduce the benefits of mechanization.

Quality requirements may impose levels of mechanization that otherwise would be uneconomical.

In some cases, large and expensive machines operated by European expatriates may be more productive than the more general plant with local operators.

Proportion of staff to labour

The level of skills and the relative ability of labour to work unsupervised determines the proportion of staff needed. Training to improve skills can cause the proportion to be changed later in the contract.

Resource levelling and optimization of labour contract periods

Imported labour should be obtained on a contract basis for durations which are a minimum of one year for training and taxation reasons.

The amount of labour needed to meet the programme has to be considered in order to try to optimize labour contract periods. Resource levelling also may have to be studied in order to allow scarce skills to be concentrated on critical path activities.

The demobilization of labour should also be part of the resource plan.

Recruitment arrangements

Recruitment from third countries can pose particular problems.

- Labour agents and brokers (if employed) need to be carefully vetted as they can pay lip service to the skill and ability of the labour supplied but merely supply those people from whom they can obtain the largest commission.

- A contract with a labour agent should withhold part of the payment until each person supplied has completed a test period of three months on site.

- An examination of the agent's operations should be made if he has not been used in the past, and references should be taken up from previous customers.

- Trade testing facilities should be set up or otherwise arranged in the countries of recruitment.

- The labour agent's activities should be spot-checked and audited regularly.

- During any intensive recruitment period, there should be a continuous presence of members of the company's staff at the recruitment offices, if possible.

Recruitment of labour and local staff within a developing country usually has a political dimension. A number of factors are usually significant.

- *tribal membership.* It may be inadvisable to have supervisors and labour from different tribes.

- *membership of political parties.* The ruling party or faction may impose screening on recruitment, in these ways.

o *local preferment.* There may be a number of placements the local 'godfather' wants to make. For good local relationships, it may be necessary to comply.

o *trades unions.* In developing countries, these are not normally of the same nature as at home. In many countries they do not really represent the work-force, but are an extension of the ruling political party. In some they are concessions granted to former 'freedom fighters', who thereby operate as labour barons. Whatever form they take, they cannot be ignored, and

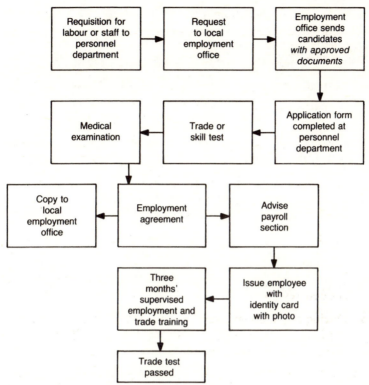

Fig. 16. Employment procedure

knowledge of their rules and methods of operations needs to be obtained.

The early appointment of a local labour officer is essential. He may be a former trade union official, a political *placeman*, or a former police or military officer.

The employment procedure for local staff and labour should include aptitude or skill testing, a period of probation, and a training period. This is shown in Fig. 16.

Conditions of employment

Information on local conditions of employment should be obtained from the appropriate ministry. Local advice will also be needed on how these are interpreted. Moreover, it is usual for the Client, who will also be a large employer, to wish to confirm general acceptability of such conditions.

The following check-list covers the more normal aspects

- normal working hours
- minimum wages
- allowances
- travelling time (especially if being collected/returned by site transport)
- overtime rates (for Sundays and equivalents, public holidays etc.)
- annual holidays and public holidays
- termination procedure
- redundancy procedure
- severance pay
- workman's compensation and/or state pension fund
- allowable deductions from pay
- ration allowance, or normal feeding options
- union dues (if collected by employers)
- union membership (closed shop etc.)
- taxation
- trade testing.

Special local requirements may apply to the termination of employment. In some countries this is difficult to achieve. It often results in the political placements being there until the end, with a subsequent loss of productivity in the run-down period.

These considerations may be of such significance that labour is not recruited by the company at all, but contracts are placed with labour-only subcontractors. Alternatively, it may be advisable to plan for the final run-down stages of the project to be carried out by subcontractors.

Third-country recruitment

Importing labour from outside the territory will still involve government regulations. These will undoubtedly relate to import quotas, residence and work permits.

In the Middle East, in countries where substantially all the labour force is imported, there may be established conditions of labour contracts which have to be complied with. There may also be conditions of employment required by the exporting country.

In the importation of labour, standards of accommodation and feeding must be clearly stated. While accommodation will be substandard from a European viewpoint, it must be adequate to maintain the labour force as an efficient unit. This should require consideration of

- numbers to a dormitory
- national and religious separation
- air-conditioning
- personal maintenance facilities
- recreation, including transport.

In the Middle East, labour from the Indian subcontinent are avid cinema-goers.

If there is no public transport available to such recreation, transport may have to be provided. Alternatively, concessions may be given to outsiders to operate cinemas on or near the camp site. This question of concessions may also extend to the provision of shopping facilities.

Feeding

Feeding is a matter of prime concern. It is inadvisable to leave the labour force to look after themselves. Usually they can do it more cheaply themselves, but usually this leads them into being underfed and underproductive.

Arranging feeding may require separate kitchens and separate food for different ethnic and religious elements of the labour force.

Labour discipline and control

Labour discipline and control relates to activities both on site and off site.

On site

On-site control involves

- initial registration of labour
- allocation of labour to gangs and to work areas
- identification, by
o tags
o clock card numbers
- timekeeping procedures.

Decisions have to be made as to whether the timekeeping procedures should be integrated with the cost control system and whether they should be computerized.

Apart from clocking on and off, the employment of roving timekeepers making spot checks should be considered. It should be borne in mind that most very large projects in the Third World will have labour forces of more than 1000 men.

On a large site, a decision has to be made on whether clocking on and off takes place centrally or whether it is in each work area. If it is in the work areas, is travelling time allowed? What are the travelling arrangements? Are there to be meal breaks? Are they taken at the work site or do they allow for the use of a central canteen?

Off site

Off-site discipline relates only to imported labour. Here it is necessary to have a member of staff identified to be responsible for off-site discipline. He may be the camp manager. He may be of any nationality, but he should speak the principal language of the labour force.

Labour officer

If recruitment has been carried out by the company using its own personnel, the labour officer associated with this would be an obvious candidate as the discipline officer.

This officer should establish contacts with the local police and security organization, and set up procedures for dealing with problems, including repatriating offenders. All such procedures require to be referred to in the labour contracts.

Where an indigenous labour force is involved, it is advisable to recruit a retired member of the local police or security organizations to act as the labour officer generally responsible for discipline. Of course, at the actual work site the normal project command structure should apply, but the labour officer may be required to assist from time to time.

If there is trade union representation on site, the labour officer should interface with its senior representative and establish a liaison committee.

Payment

A decision has to be made on the method and frequency of paying the labour force. Payment on a fortnightly basis is quite normal.

The integration of the payment system through the payroll with the timekeeping and the costing system has to be considered. Security is an aspect in this. It is advisable to have sufficient duplication in the system to allow for cross-checking. The degree of computerization has to be decided.

With a large labour force and dependence on indigenous and imported third-country staff in timekeeping and payment clerical functions, cross-checking and regular security inspections must be made. The staff in these functions as far as possible should be protected from pressure to collude with operatives for the purpose of fraud.

Safety

A member of the expatriate staff should be appointed as safety officer. He should head a committee including the labour officer and the trade union representative if there is one on site. In the absence of this, a member of the labour force should be appointed and also a local staff representative.

Safety regulations in force in the country must be applied. In the absence of these, or to supplement them, a model set of regulations should be established for the site, drawing on home experience. Safety should be considered as a means of improving overall productivity and should be included as a subject in the site training programme.

Figure 17 shows the impact of a special set of safety courses on the accident statistics of a major project in Asia.

Safety statistics should be kept and results published. There

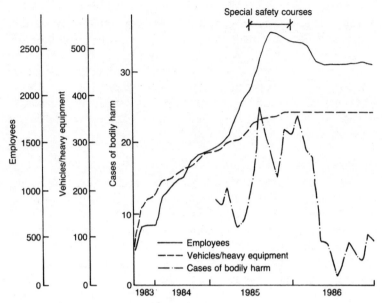

Fig. 17. Impact of safety courses on the accident statistics of a major project in Asia

should be campaigns to increase safety awareness. Normally accidents result largely from low skills and training levels, and in a Third World country there is even greater possibility of them happening than at home. The results will be at least as damaging as at home to progress of the works.

Safety equipment must always be available. Lack of it will discourage observance by the labour force.

Medical facilities

The medical facilities referred to for staff (chapter 7) should also be available to the labour force.

A clinic or hospital at the expatriate camp should provide emergency hospital services and it should be designed with sufficient capacity for this. First aid equipment and accommodation should be provided on site, and an ambulance should be kept there to transfer serious accident cases either to the clinic or to the nearest hospital. A trained first aid man or men must also be on site during working hours.

Obviously, the extent of the risks of exposure to injury should determine the level of medical facilities to be made available. Tunnelling has the greatest level of risk.

Training

Training and technology transfer is usually an important aspect of any project placed with foreign contractors in a developing country, and a training programme may form part of the contract. Even where this is not the case, training must be viewed as an important aspect of site productivity.

The training programme should be tailored to suit a low initial skill and knowledge base. The programme should contain as many simple illustrations and demonstrations as practical. The detail should not only concentrate on the basic job in hand, but should also relate it to associated tasks and provide a background of understanding of the rationale behind the task.

Accidents are usually caused through lack of real awareness of the risks inherent in many simple repetitive operations, and knowledge needs to be imparted on how things might go wrong.

Case study

A major hydroelectric project in Asia, where a training and technology transfer programme formed part of the contract, is taken as a case study. The training described here is for construction staff and operatives. Engineers and operators of the installed plant were trained separately at the plant suppliers' premises and at specially designed courses in Europe and Indonesia. Training also featured during commissioning and handover.

Table 4. Numbers trained and retrained

Vocational and skill training	2581
Safety courses	617
Advanced vocational training	108
Courses for supervisors and foremen	130
Site management courses for senior local staff, including Client's	16
Overseas executive training programme for Client's managers	4

Table 5. Course for training of operators

Requirements for admission to the course
Driving licence for car
Certificate from the police showing a clean driving record
Required medical certificate for driving a motor vehicle
Either passing of driving test according to the directions of the training manager *or* passing of drivers' course to the satisfaction of the training manager

Course participants
Nine men per course

Course programme
Theoretical vocational training, 1 week; practical vocational training, 2 weeks; vocational work, 3 weeks

Theoretical stage: basic knowledge of running, tipping, loading, maintenance and handling of excavators, dozers and wheel loaders; safety regulations; the course leader and one instructor will be responsible; during certain lessons, well-qualified teachers from suppliers of loading vehicles will assist

Practical stage: the trainees will be divided into three groups (bulldozers, excavators, wheel loaders) and directed by three instructors

Vocational work: application of theoretical and practical knowledge in connection with tunnel driving and other civil engineering work; safety precautions; one instructor will be responsible

Contents of theoretical stage
Presentation of the course: general information on and aim of the course

Engines and machinery: general information on excavators, wheel loaders and dozers; motors, construction and method of operation; cooling system; lubrication system; fuel system; electrical equipment; air, oil and fuel filters; power transmission, clutch and gearbox; frame, wheels and axles; steering system; brake system; hydraulic equipment; wearing parts; tyres; other attachments; scoop attachments

Service and maintenance: cleaning of plant and machines; checking and maintenance according to instruction books; fuels, lubrication and oil change; spare parts and accessories; simple repairs; tracing trouble; labour welfare

Test and examination of test

---

continued on facing page

Table 5 — continued

Contents of practical stage

Instruction on plant operation: planning and preparation of different routines; control and function of steering unit; safety precautions in connection with particular work; starting practice; position of vehicle during work; manoeuvring of scoop and blade; moving of vehicle during work; special practice runnings

swinging and emptying when loading; face and trench excavation	especially for excavator operators
carrying out of simple loading and levelling, driving with markers, loading blasted rock in tunnels	especially for wheel-loader operators
carrying out simple levelling; top soil removal; driving with markers; slopes and terraces for roads and dam profiles	especially for bulldozer operators

Practical servicing, maintenance and repairs: cleaning of plant and machines; checking and maintenance according to instruction books; wrecking; simple repairs, tracing trouble

Oil, lubricants and fuels: information and description of oils, lubricants and fuels; handling, safety regulations

Temporary electrical installations: short description of definitions and demands; safety regulations

Dewatering: general information on dewatering; pumps and pipes

Ventilation: demands, pipe systems and fans

Pneumatic engines: design and function; attendance and range of application

Air inlet control: design, function and attendance

Loading vehicles: design and function

Pneumatic lights and pumps: design and function; attendance

Engine drilling machines and pneumatic breakers: general information

Safety and environment: ergonomy, noise, gases, vibrations etc.; local stipulations

Test and examination of test

Film

Training of construction operatives and staff at various levels was carried out as shown in Table 4. All the labour force had been through at least one training course.

The advanced vocational training course was carried out by four teachers from a technical college in the country. The site management course was carried out by company personnel, assisted by three internationally trained consultants.

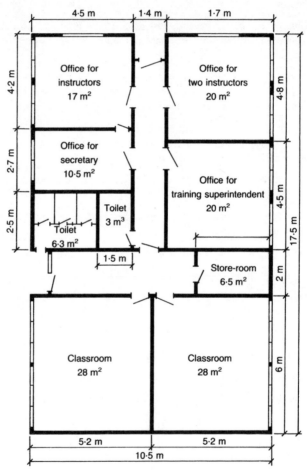

Fig. 18. School building layout

Table 5 shows a typical vocational training plan, in this case for plant operators.

Training was carried out principally on site, although a selected number of the Client's senior managers were sent to courses in Europe.

The layout of the training school building on site is shown in Fig. 18 and the basic classroom equipment in Table 6. Textbooks and training material essentially consisted of maintenance manuals and suppliers' brochures supplemented by material prepared by the instructors.

The staff of the school was headed by an expatriate training superintendent who reported to the plant manager. The training superintendent was also the site safety officer.

Under the training superintendent were four instructors who, later in the project, after training and development periods, were locally employed. At the beginning of the project all the principal plant suppliers made instructors available. On average, expatriate instructors were used during the first two years of the five-year contract period.

Table 6. Classroom equipment

3	tables	1	Polaroid Lightmixer 630 camera
9	tables, locally made	1	Polaroid Miniportrait camera
2	tables,short		+ Crown Quick 175 light
6	tables, long	1	Olympus camera
5	cupboards, steel	1	tripod
2	cupboards, wood	1	pan
13	bookselves	1	pair of binoculars
7	chairs, rotary	1	empty video cassette E180
32	chairs, red	2	white boards
2	chairs, wooden	1	Da-lite film screen
1	filing cabinet	2	stands for projector
1	calculator, Sharp	1	stand for writing pad
7	air conditioners	1	stand for picture
1	refrigerator	1	bench
1	electric pot	1	vernier callipers
1	EIKI film projector	1	tape recorder — Hanimex
1	Kodak slide projector		2040 AV
1	cabin overhead projector		

The course durations were as shown in Table 7. Retraining occurred as well as training.

Benefit of training

It is difficult to assess fully the benefit of training. There was clear evidence in this case that safety improved dramatically due to the specialist safety courses and the generally improved awareness

Table 7. Course durations

Course	Hours
Bulldozer operators	100
Motor grader operators	100
Excavator operators	104
Wheel loader operators	104
Crane operators	79
Forklift operators	105
Compaction roller operators	79
Mobile concrete pump operators	99
Dump truck operators	100
Truck drivers	100
Transmixer drivers	100
Light vehicle drivers	18
Farm tractor drivers	72
Drillers and blasters	24
Concrete workers	6
Reinforcement bar workers	3
Carpenters	10
Scaffolders	30
Plant mechanics	72
Service station mechanics	24
Crushing plant operators and mechanics	35
Site electricians	72
Site management	
Basic	109
Intermediate	120
Advanced	240
Storekeeping induction course	25
Supervisors and foremen	30
Various safety courses	3

of risks. There was a view that productivity had increased as a result of training, but there was no available measure for this.

There was a subjective attempt by site supervisors to analyse the improvements against a range of topics for a number of samples. Of a total potential score of 60 points, the average for the samples was 20 points, which represented on the scoring mechanism that the training on average had a moderately significant influence on performance. The effects that were most highly rated were on

- skill
- interest
- ability to work unsupervised
- reduction of accidents
- treatment of plant.

Productivity was considered to have been only moderately improved. The training was considered not to have had any influence on attendance or absence from work.

The particular difficulty in the case was to get expatriate supervisors who had any ability to train. In this the case fell short of expectations. In recruiting expatriates, this is a factor that must be considered.

9 Materials and subcontractors

Materials and subcontractors are dealt with in this chapter because both involve procurement processes. Construction plant is dealt with in chapter 10, because the important aspect of asset management puts this in a separate category.

The principal aspects of purchasing and shipping are dealt with here, but those that are peculiar to the procurement of plant and spare parts are referred to in chapter 10.

The relationships needed between company departments and the project organization to procure materials and subcontractors are shown in Fig. 19.

Materials

The supply of materials is analysed under the following headings

- resource planning
- indenting
- enquiries and purchasing
- inspection
- expediting
- packing and shipping
- port clearance and inland transport
- storage and issue.

Resource planning

The supply of materials to a Third World project normally involves slow communications and lengthy deliveries. Scheduling of materials has to take into account

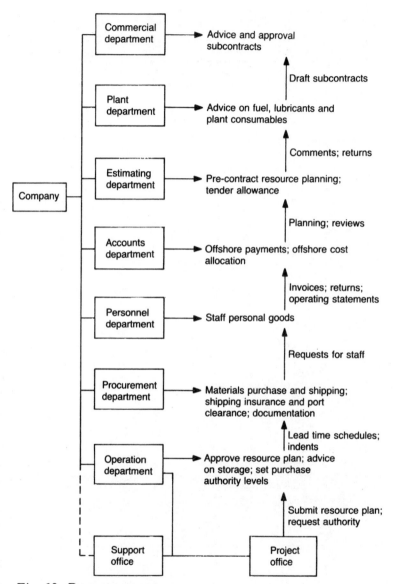

Fig. 19. Procurement sequence

Material	Req. No.	Approved drawings issued by			Requisition by			Order by			Manufacture by			Ship by			On site by			Remarks
		Earliest	Latest	Actual	Earliest	Latest	Actual	Earliest	Latest	Actual	Earliest	Latest	Actual	Earliest	Latest	Actual	Earliest	Latest	Actual	

Fig. 20. Procurement control schedule

- manufacturers' delivery times to a packing station or seaport
- sea freight times
- port clearance times
- inland transport times.

If documents have to be translated into the local language, further time must be allowed.

Normally, three months is a minimum for materials to reach site. For some items, 4–6 months is not unusual. This results in the need to hold stocks for longer than would be normal at home. Careful control of their use and of wastage is necessary, so that emergency air-freighting of replacements or additions is avoided. Equally, the writing-off of surplus stocks at the end of the contract must be minimized.

Air-freighting is a costly alternative to shipping, and if there are delays in airport clearance caused by the formalities and procedures it is not necessarily an immediate service. In a developing country it is unwise to assume that an air-freighted article will be delivered in less than one month from the date of ordering.

Vendor list

The initial step in resource planning is to prepare a vendor list for all the principal materials and supplies. This should have been initiated during the tender period but will need updating at the start of the contract.

The vendor list should state alternative suppliers for the main items. It should give information on required delivery time, price and specification. These will all have to be revalidated by specific quotations.

Lead time schedule

From the vendor list and the master programme, a lead time schedule is prepared as shown in Table 8. From this, the latest dates for inviting enquiries can be flagged up in the procurement control schedule (Fig. 20).

The items that have to be taken into consideration in preparing the lead time schedule and the procurement control schedules are

- the requisition-by date: the date that the requisition must be received by the home office (if issued by site) and the date it must be completed if prepared in the home office

- the order-by date: the date the order must be issued, allowing for
- checking of the requisition by the procurement department
- clarification of ambiguities in a requisition raised by the procurement department or the vendor
- time to issue enquiries
- receipt of offers and negotiation with vendors
- production of enquiry comparisons
- obtaining and approval of samples as necessary
- selection of the vendor
- preparation and placement of the order

- the manufacture-by date, allowing for
- preparation and approval of specification/working drawings
- ordering and delivery of materials/equipment
- receipt of vendor data and approval
- manufacture/test period
- inspection period
- packing

- the ship-by date, allowing for
- frequency (or infrequency) of sailings to landing port
- delivery to UK docks
- clearance and loading at UK docks
- delay before sailing after ship closes
- sailing time
- delay due to port congestion at landing port
- unloading and clearance at landing port
- delivery to site.

Indenting

A purchase is initiated by an indent being raised. This can be done by the project office at site, the liaison office or the home-based support office. Whichever route is taken, all indents must be uniquely numbered and a control file of all indents must be kept at the project office.

The indent should provide the basic information required to initiate enquiry procedures. It should include the data on the procurement control schedule if it relates to principal material purchases. If it represents materials required by the project stores to make up stocks, it should have the stores reference information and when delivery to site is required. If plant spares are involved, machine descriptions and relevant serial numbers should be included.

The indent should state the cost allocation code.

Any special requirements such as inspection should be clearly shown in the indent and the method of delivery should also be stated.

Indents should also be used for calling off material deliveries which have been the subject of a bulk order.

Indents should state urgency. Care should be taken to avoid all indents having the greatest urgency stated.

Enquiries and purchasing

Enquiries should be issued to preselected vendors in accordance with the company or joint venture procedure. The procedure will include the number of quotations to be sought.

For some materials, an updating of vendor files may be all that is necessary, if the information in these files is extensive and up to date.

Enquiries should be numbered and referenced to the relevant indents, and an enquiry control file should be maintained at the site office.

A post code should be included in every enquiry.

For most developing-country projects, it is likely that shipping will be organized by the project support office, and not by suppliers and vendors. The suppliers and vendors should be asked to deliver to a packing station or to the port. If there are any special packing or shipping instructions these should also be included in an enquiry.

A requirement for a fixed price or an escalation-payment formula should be clearly stated. The payment terms, including currencies, should be stated.

The technical specification should be detailed. If alternatives are allowed or if the specification has to be provided by the vendor, this should be stated in the enquiry.

Bonding and guarantee requirements should be stated.

Quality assurance procedures should be described.

Bid summaries

The following should be stated in a bid summary

- budget/tender price
- quotation price
- packing/shipping costs
- inspection and expediting costs
- gain or loss on budget
- delivery situation
- payment terms
- compliance with specification or alternative specification
- time to get approval of alternative specification
- date when order should be placed
- enquiry file numbers
- cost codes.

Orders

An order should be placed only after final details have been agreed with the vendor, including

- programme and delivery sequence (this must detail the manufacturing programme or the supplier's queuing sequence and procedure for individual items to work their way through the queue)
- a requirement to report progress on a regular basis against manufacturing or queuing dates
- any conditions that need mutual agreement.

Also, approvals required from the Client or Engineer must have been obtained.

Orders should provide the following information

- drawings and specification, including approval procedure for working drawings
- bonds, guarantees and warranties

	Order No. ....
Delivery instructions	*Application for instructions should be made at the earliest opportunity to our Shipping Agents named below.*
Packing instructions	Goods must be securely packed and protected for ocean shipment and inland transit to Site or packed suitably for UK transport to our Export Packer as noted on our order.
Shipping marks	All packages and documents must be clearly and indelibly marked as below, with the other forming part of the shipping mark. ....
Shipping agent	....
Invoices . . . copies to company . . . copies to Shipping Agent . . . Copies to	Must be in the name of .... and include (i) Order number as above. (ii) Shipping mark as above. (iii) Shipment details (if available). (iv) CCN Main Section Codes against the goods supplied. (v) A statement of value and country of origin. (vi) Full decription of all goods, prices and discounts of each item supplied. (vii) All outside dimensions together with individual net and gross weights of each package, *in metric values*. If these are not shown, port authorities will measure all packages and their expenses will be charged to your account. (viii) *Need not show VAT as this order is for export from the UK.* (ix) Must be 'certified true and correct' and signed by an Officer of your Company.
Description of goods	The exact description of all goods supplied is essential information for all export documents. HM Custom and Port Authorities will not accept the words 'package' or 'packages'. Precise descriptions must be shown, i.e. 'cartons', 'crates', 'bundles', 'loose' etc.
Shipping notes Copy to company	Your shipping note lodged with the Port Authority at the port of shipment must agree in every respect with that on all other documents and with the goods supplied.
FOB charges *(where applicable)*	Must include all dock dues and charges irrespective of the custom of the port.
Marine insurance	Not required. (We will arrange.)
Legalized and/or *consular invoices*	If required, will be arranged by us.
Special instructions *(if any)*	....

Fig. 21. Shipping instructions

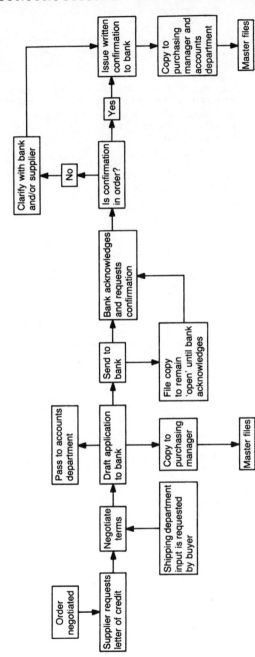

Only senior purchasing officers and above may issue drafts to accounts for onward transmission to bank.

Fig. 22. Letters of credit flow chart: all letters of credit are post-dated pre-conditioned cheques; irrevocable letters of credit will be paid by the bank on due presentation of documents only; no check is made of goods physically (recommended reading — 'Guide to documentary credit operations', published by the International Chamber of Commerce)

o type, payment, performance
o on demand?
o surety?
o duration
o procedure for delivery

● programme and expediting information

● delivery
o ex works
o free on board (FOB): named port or packing station
o free alongside (FAS): named vessel
o shipping instructions where appropriate (see Fig. 21)

● payment
o documents required
o letters of credit etc. (see Fig. 22)
o bills of lading
o certificates of value and origin of goods: legalizing procedure
  for documents and payment advances

● insurance: arranged by vendor or customer

● requirements for samples

● other documents

● reference to indent numbers

● cost code

● related correspondence

● document control procedure

● free supply materials.

Inspection

Inspection should be carried out as part of the quality assurance procedure for the project. Auditing of the quality assurance procedure should be separate from inspection.

Inspection should be carried out in accordance with an inspection/expediting programme for the project. This programme should be based on the procurement control schedule and the manufacturers' programmes.

| Expediting rating: | Critical Needs watching satisfactory | ☐ ☐ ☐ | | Inspection rating: | Very good Average Poor | ☐ ☐ ☐ | | Works loading: | Heavy Medium Light | ☐ ☐ ☐ |

Main order No.	Vendor and location	Tel. No.
Sub order No.	Sub-vendor and location	Tel. No.
Vendor's ref.	Contact	

Equipment/material on order

Drawings/specifications used

General progress

Last visit date		This visit date				Next visit date		
Item No.	Required delivery	Last promise	Current promise	Expected delivery	% Drgs complete	% Drgs approved	Weld proc. approved	% material received	% manufact. complete

Details of expediting/inspection visit

Action

Code/specification complies	Yes/No	Test satisfactory	Yes/No	Further visit	Yes/No
Despatch released	Yes/No	Release note number			
Expeditor's signature Checked by Chief Expeditor		Inspecting Engineer's signature Checked by Chief Inspector			

Fig. 23. Inspection and expediting report form

The programme should cover all materials that are vital to the progress of the works and should specify the following dates

- start of manufacture

- completion of manufacture

- completion of parts (interim dates) (also location of manufacture should be given)

- delivery to loading port or packing station.

From the programme, the dates for individual inspection visits should be identified and agreed with the vendor. The dates when deliveries of samples and test pieces are due should also be shown in the programme.

The inspection visits should also serve expediting needs. A typical inspection and expediting report form is shown in Fig. 23. The inspectors should receive copies of all the correspondence and minutes of meetings relevant to the materials to be inspected.

Before delivery of goods is accepted, a note confirming acceptability by the inspectors must be received by the procurement department. This should be on a standard form.

Expediting

At the earliest opportunity after the placement of a purchase order, the expediting department should contact the vendor

- to ensure that vendor has received order

- to confirm delivery promises

- to ensure that all information needed to complete the order is in hand

- to ensure that sub-orders have been placed, or determine when they will be

- to ensure that drawing office resources have been allocated

- to ensure that manufacturing space has been allocated

- if the materials are batch-produced, to establish when in the manufacturing queue

- to establish a procedure for reporting progress.

The expediting department should monitor progress by receiving regular reports from the vendor. The physical checking of these reports by the customer's inspectors should be incorporated into the procedure for field inspections.

The expediting department should monitor the document control procedure associated with and stated in the order, to ensure that the information needed by the vendor, including routine approvals, is always made available in time.

All expediting and inspection reports should be sent to the support office for forwarding to the project office.

Packing and shipping

When inspectors confirm that material is approved for shipment, the suppliers should telex the shipping department with a full packing specification and contents list. If the company is to arrange the export packing, the supplier should notify the shipping department of the item order numbers and the quantities available.

The shipping department should issue call-forward instructions against a vessel booking reference to the packing station, with copies to the suppliers. The procedure after this should be as follows.

- The packers notify the shipping department when goods received.

- The shipping office advises packers of the intended vessel, arrangements for sending forward, consignment reference numbers — to which all documents should refer — and supply marks.

- The packers provide the shipping department with a copy of the manifest for each container.

- Where the goods are packed but not containerized, the shipping department advises the supplier of the intended vessel and provides the consignment reference and shipping marks.

- When the shipping department has received the container manifest or packing details, the following documents are produced
  o packing list (corresponding with bill of lading)
  o invoice
  o certificate of origin

o draft bill of lading

- The certificate of origin has to be legalized by the embassy of the host country.

- The port authorities advise when packages are delivered.

- The legalized certificate of origin is checked against the packages at port awaiting shipment. When correct, the shipping company is instructed to proceed with loading.

- The shipping department submits finalized bill of lading to the shipping company.

- The shipping department sends a telex to the project office via the support office giving
o invoice number
o cost insurance and freight (CIF) value
o number of packages
o total weight in kilograms

- The shipping department completes the insurance certificate.

- The day the vessel sails, the shipping department collects signed original bills of lading from the shipping company.

- The shipping department sends a further telex to the project office with the additional information on bills of lading numbers and dates.

- The shipping department sends by courier five sets of documents to the project office.
o The first set is for the customs and comprises the original bill of lading, original commercial invoice, packing list, legalized certificate of origin and original certificate of marine insurance.
o Four photocopied sets are normally sent to the project office for the Client, the Engineer, project records and project stores.

- The shipping department sends a telex to the project office advising details of the courier despatch.

- One set of copies of the documents above is sent separately by courier to the clearing agent at the port of arrival.

- The shipping department sends a telex to the clearing agent advising details of the courier despatch.

- Three copies of the insurance certificate are sent to the insurance company as soon as possible.

- If requested, a copy of the bill of lading or a certificate of shipment is sent to the supplier for VAT purposes.

- The shipping department sends to the accounts department a copy of each freight account certified for payment.

- Each supplier's invoice is checked against the purchase order, certified for payment and sent to the accounts department.

- The shipping department should comply with UK customs procedures for export of goods.

- The project office advises the shipping office of the arrival of goods, confirming the date of arrival and any damage or discrepancy.

- The shipping office deals with any discrepancies or insurance claims.

An abbreviated version of the above procedure should be completed for air freight. For this, the despatch of original documents for customs clearance becomes critical to avoid delays.

Port clearance and inland transport

Port clearance should be organized through a clearing agent in the port of delivery, who should be responsible for compliance with all customs formalities and should make such arrangements as are necessary within the port for goods to be taken from the dockside, stored as necessary, and loaded on inland transport.

In some authorities, all handling within the port has to be done by the port authorities. In others it is restricted to registered contractors. In some, the company may have to provide the labour and cranage.

Inland transport may be by the company's own vehicles or by local transport contractors.

As marine insurance covers the goods until they are over the ship's rail, appropriate insurance has to be organized within the country for the port clearance and inland transport. If own transport is used, the site insurance should be extended to cover the transport of goods off site.

Storage and issue

Storage of materials within a developing country has much greater importance than within the home base. To a large extent, a project must be self-supporting. In some countries very little can be obtained from the locality.

The range of goods to be obtained and stored may therefore have to be very comprehensive, and retrieval and ordering systems must ensure that goods are always available when needed, but that there is the minimum of stock. Staff should be carefully trained.

Stores organization

The stores should be managed by an expatriate, who should be at the third level of command of the project. This person may well be running the equivalent of a building supply company with a turnover of more than £10 million a year.

The size of the stores staff should reflect the amount of work in the four main storekeeping functions

- receipt of materials

- central recording and maintenance of stock levels

- issues

- continuous audit.

Receipt of materials

There must be a stores check-point to which all vehicles delivery materials report.

The checking and acceptance procedure should be the same whether supplies to site are procured locally or shipped from overseas.

Approved forms should be used for

- goods-received tickets

- materials-received record sheets.

Bulk materials that are to be delivered to locations other than the central stores require special procedures. Goods-received tickets should be issued by field checkers and these may also be accompanied by weighbridge tickets. If there is no weighbridge on site, or if the materials are not suitable for weighbridge checking,

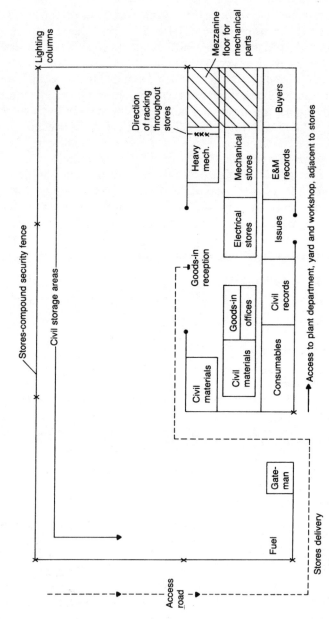

Fig. 24. Typical layout of site stores and stores compound

the field checker must make sure that sufficient check measurements are carried out, either in the vehicle or after unloading.

All goods-received tickets should be entered in the materials-received record sheet. If possible, the cost allocation code should be included in the record. The record should also state the order number. The location of the materials within the store or on site should be included in the materials-received record.

Information should be transferred from the materials-received record sheet, which is in fact a daybook, to individual record sheets for each item. This should state the materials-received record number and the order number. These record sheets should also record issues and stock levels.

Stores layout

A typical stores layout is shown in Fig. 24.

A check-list for establishing a central stores would include the following items.

- The site storage compound must be of adequate size, located on open ground and adjacent to the plant workshop and fabrication shops. The stores building should be of adequate size and secure. Ideally, the location should only be settled after consideration of the following.

o The compound should be as near as possible to the 'centre of gravity' of the site to avoid the need for too many secondary stores.

o It should face the site access road.

o It should not be adjacent to the site car park.

o It should be fenced and hardcored.

o It should be convenient for site services.

o There should be access to the store for both incoming vehicles and site staff.

o The goods-received area should be at the opposite end of the stores building from the issues area.

o The compound should be secure from potential flooding.

o Siting of the compound should not cause obstruction immediately outside the site or to the public.

o There should be adequate space for the plant workshop to be located next door to the stores building.

o The availability of planning permission for the building should be considered.

● A logical location system for goods should be used, based on sequential numbering of racks, rows, columns and shelves.

● A well planned racking system should be used, such as the Dexion Maxi range.

● All site materials must be stored within the stores compound and properly accounted for by stock cards, except possibly
o bulk materials and aggregates
o special bulk containers for fuel, cement, explosives etc.
o heavy-lift individual items
o piles and trench supports (properly protected)
o pipes in a proper pipeyard
o reinforcement, properly stacked and accessible
o timber securely stored within the joiners' shop
o secondary stores (e.g. at remote locations or quarry) and separate stores for office supplies and medical stores

● Before the use of a material dump outside the storage compound is planned and authorized, the following should be considered.
o Is the dump essential or could be eliminated by arranging a different delivery schedule? If not, how permanent is it to be?
o Is it in public view?
o Is it accessible for deliveries and withdrawals?
o Is it adjacent to the user section to avoid double handling?
o Are the ground conditions suitable?
o Are necessary storage aids available?
o Can planning permission be obtained?

● Adequate materials handling and transport equipment should be provided.

Stock-recording systems

Each item in the stores or in site storage should have a stock record card. The Kardex system is well tried in developing-country situations, using type A for fast-moving items and type B for slower-moving items. This system can be substituted by use of computers if this is considered suitable. On a major project, the stores may need to stock 5000–10 000 items. Kardex provides 72 cards per tray and twelve trays per cabinet. Therefore some ten cabinets would be required for this level of stockholding. The Kardex stock cards are altered from information on the materials-received record sheets and the indent on stores. Stock cards may also be altered by using transfer vouchers if materials are relocated or if there are errors.

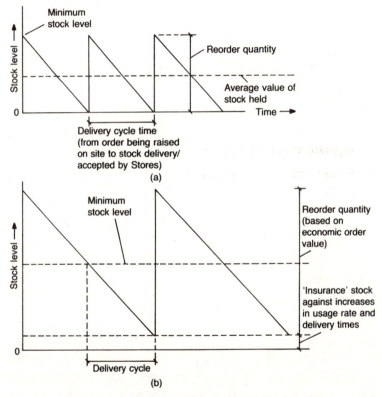

Fig. 25. Maximum–minimum stock control: (a) ideal (and impractical) stockholding; the average value of stock held is half the minimum stock level and the reorder quantity is equal to the minimum stock level; (b) typical situation; the minimum stock level is increased from that determined by the delivery cycle by an amount of insurance; stock value (average) is half the reorder quantity plus the insurance value

Stock control

Some materials may be controlled on a maximum–minimum stock level basis, so that reordering is automatically triggered by the stock level report. The mechanism is shown in Fig. 25. The levels should be set according to the relationship between rate of usage and delivery time, including time to get through customs.

Apart from the maximum–minimum stock level control procedure, materials stock should be controlled through a weekly check by the project planning staff. Statistics of stock use and holdings should be produced regularly, on a monthly, bi-monthly or six-monthly basis, depending on usage profiles.

Issue procedures

Materials should be issued only against the authorization of an indent on stores. Each indent should include reference to

● material identity

● quantity

● section of works

● cost allocation

● authority.

Returned materials are treated as new materials from a recording point of view.

Information systems

Physical quantity reconciliations should be carried out on bulk materials.

Cost reports should include receipts to stores, issues from stores, stock levels and allocations to work sections against cost codes. Physical stock checks should be carried out at six-monthly intervals.

A report on stock held should be made annually and a review of potential stock write-offs should be made.

Subcontractors

The procedure for requesting a subcontractor should be the same as that for indenting for materials. It should be arranged through the support office for offshore subcontractors and through the project office for onshore subcontractors.

The invitation to tender for a subcontract should state the following

- description of work
- time to bid
- bid documents, including form of contract
- programme for subcontract work
- payment terms
- bonds
- free issues and facilities
- local regulations
- insurance.

If possible, a standard form of subcontract should be used, unless this is contrary to local commercial culture. Overformality should be avoided in appointing local subcontractors if this is against the culture. Conditions of contract should not be imposed which are unlikely to be applied in practice.

Care should be taken in giving local subcontractors a detailed briefing and in examining their capability of performing the works.

The procedure for placing subcontractors should comply with the company's rules for home-based operations, though with modifications for local commercial practice in the case of local subcontracts.

Local legal opinion should be sought both on the form of subcontract and the method of obtaining performance. While it may seem advisable to retain adequate sums of money against performance, local subcontractors may not have the financial capacity to withstand this.

Subcontracts should not be placed locally for any work which is critical to the programme or performance of the works.

Until equipment is available and labour has been recruited, it may be necessary to have advance works carried out by subcontractors. Adequate float should be allowed in programmes for this.

There may be political reasons for employing local subcontractors. Also, as stated previously, conditions for employing labour may be onerous, and labour-only subcontracting may be a preferred alternative.

It may be impossible for local subcontractors to obtain insurance for their works and this should be provided for in the overall works policies.

10 Construction plant

Construction plant is considered under four headings

- purchasing and shipping

- maintenance and spares

- asset management

- disposal.

The relationships needed between company departments and the project organization to provide construction plant are shown in Fig. 26.

Purchasing and delivery
The selection of plant for a large project in a developing country should depend on

- the nature of the work to be carried out

- previous experience

- price

- robustness needed

- back-up

- compatibility

- availability

In most developing countries not much plant is available for hire, if any. Care must be taken to avoid delays due to lack of plant availability. Machinery should be as compatible as possible to limit the range of spares that have to be stored.

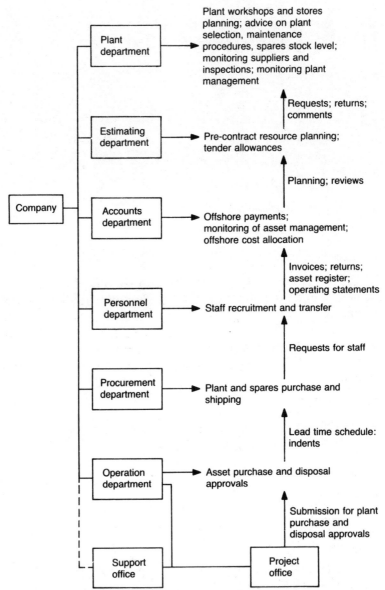

Fig. 26. Plant selection, procurement and maintenance sequence

Plant selection should be based on the tender plant schedule. From this and the project master programme, a plant programme should be produced covering all major plant. This should incorporate all current planning decisions.

Lead time schedule

A lead time schedule, similar to that shown in Table 8 for materials, should be produced. Some of the column headings will be different, but the principles are the same.

Plant purchasing represents the acquisition of major assets, unlike material purchases which can be initiated by a simple indenting procedure. Companies and joint ventures should therefore have specific procedures for the purchasing of plant, which may involve approval by senior directors or even the main boards of the companies involved.

The information that is presented for approval, either in or with the lead time schedule, should include

- price of item
- normal life in hours
- expected hours utilized on project
- expected resale value (guaranteed buy back by supplier if possible)
- depreciation allowed in tender
- outright purchase or leasing arrangements
- warranties
- plant supplier's local agents.

The company's plant department should start obtaining prices from plant suppliers as soon as the lead time schedule is completed. Summaries of these prices and proposals for purchase, together with the information listed above should then go for formal approval.

After approval has been obtained and the orders have been placed, the plant should be called forward by the project office, in accordance with the lead time schedule.

Machinery should be planned so that spares are as

Table 8. Typical lead time schedule for procurement*

Material or item	Enquiry	Analysis	Obtain and submit sample	Approve sample	Place order	Prepare and submit drawings	Approve drawings
Road signs •	20	2	20	15	1	15	20
Fencing and gates	10	2	10	15	1	10	15
Guardrail	10	2	10	15	1	—	—
Reinforcement	10	2	—	—	1	—	—
Bearing pads	—	—	—	—	—	—	—
Structural steelwork	15	3	—	—	2	15	20
Misc. metalwork	15	3	—	—	2	15	20
Expansion joints	—	—	—	—	—	—	—
Wooden windows	15	3	—	—	2	15	20
Sealants	7	2	—	—	1	—	—
Demountable partitions •	25	2	20	15	1	15	15
Toilet accessories •	25	2	20	15	1	—	—
Door hardware •	25	2	20	15	1	—	—
Blinds	10	2	10	15	1	—	—
Unit kitchens	10	2	—	—	1	10	15
Flagpoles	—	—	—	—	—	—	—
Lockers	—	—	—	—	—	—	—
Mesh partitions	10	2	—	—	1	—	—
Aluminium louvres •	25	2	—	—	1	15	15
WC partitions	—	—	—	—	—	—	—
Vinyl wallcovering •	25	2	20	15	1	—	—
Carpets •	25	2	20	15	1	—	—
Resilient flooring •	25	2	20	15	1	—	—
Metal cladding •	25	2	20	15	1	20	15
Ceilings	25	3	10	15	1	20	15
Floor and wall tiles	20	2	10	15	1	—	—
Furring and lath	10	2	—	—	1	—	—
Aluminium window walling •	25	3	20	15	1	25	20
Glass	—	—	—	—	—	—	—
Metal stud system	15	2	—	—	1	—	—
Bridge crane	15	2	—	—	1	15	15
Plaster	—	—	—	—	—	—	—
Engineering office equipment	15	2	—	—	1	—	—
Paint	15	2	—	—	1	—	—
Flashings	—	—	—	—	—	—	—
Roof-hatch	—	—	—	—	—	—	—
Skylights	15	2	—	—	1	10	20
Folding doors	15	2	—	—	1	—	—
Hollow metal doors	15	2	—	—	1	15	20
Grilles and passdoors	15	2	—	—	1	15	20
Timber doors	15	2	10	15	1	—	—
Aluminium entrance doors	15	2	15	20	1	15	20

* 5 days = 1 working week; ex = local (including Middle East) unless shown •

118

Manufact. period	Inspection period	Delivery and packing period	Invoice period	Shipping documents	Allocate and call forward	Shipping period	Lead total	
60–200	5	10	—	—	7	14	189–329	Ex Saudi
80	—	2	—	—	—	—	145	
80	—	2	—	—	—	—	120	
20–30	—	2	—	—	—	—	35–45	
—	—	—	—	—	—	—	—	
60	5	2	—	—	—	—	122	
60	5	2	—	—	—	—	122	
—	—	—	—	—	—	—	—	
20	5	2	—	—	—	—	82	
5–40	—	2	—	—	—	—	17–52	
30–40	5	10	—	—	7	42	187–197	Ex UK
40–60	5	10	—	—	7	56	181–201	Ex USA
120	5	10	—	—	7	56	261	Ex USA
20–30	5	2	—	—	—	—	65–75	
20–30	5	2	—	—	—	—	65–75	
—	—	—	—	—	—	—	—	
—	—	—	—	—	—	—	—	
10–15	5	2	—	—	—	—	30–35	
50–60	5	10	—	—	7	56	186–196	Ex USA
—	—	—	—	—	—	—	—	
15–20	—	10	—	—	7	56	151–156	Ex USA
20–30	—	10	—	—	7	56	156–166	Ex USA
30–40	—	10	—	—	7	56	166–176	Ex USA
30–40	5	10	—	—	7	56	196–216	Ex USA
30–40	5	2	—	—	—	—	126–136	
40–50	5	10	—	—	7	42	142–153	Ex Germany
20–30	—	2	—	—	—	—	35–45	
145	5	10	—	—	7	56	332	Ex USA
—	—	—	—	—	—	—	—	
20–30	—	2	—	—	—	—	40–50	
50–60	5	10	—	—	7	42	162–172	Ex France
—	—	—	—	—	—	—	—	
30–40	—	2	—	—	—	—	50–60	
10–20	—	2	—	—	—	—	40–50	
—	—	—	—	—	—	—	—	
—	—	—	—	—	—	—	—	
60	5	2	—	—	—	—	113	
20–30	—	2	—	—	—	—	40–50	
60	5	2	—	—	—	—	120	
20–60	5	2	—	—	—	—	80–120	
10–40	5	2	—	—	—	—	60–90	
60–80	5	2	—	—	—	—	155–175	

interchangeable as possible (e.g. caterpillar dozers and caterpillar generators). If the plant is procured in large quantities, it is desirable to obtain with it the services of a manufacturer's maintenance fitter for a significant period covering its start-up and initial use, while the project maintenance staff are gaining experience.

Arduous working conditions

Normally in developing countries the working conditions for plant are arduous. The following factors are often present

- overheating
- sand and grit
- salt (particularly in the Middle East)
- unsympathetic operators
- unskilled maintenance.

The potential effects of all these require a realistic prediction of broken-down time and the resulting number of units required to maintain production. It would be unrealistic to assume less than 30% broken-down time for most items of equipment that are in continuous use. This proportion will vary depending on whether or not there is extensive double-shift working and how long the plant will remain in the territory.

For a major project lasting three years or more, it is advisable to buy new all major items of equipment that are going to be subject to continuous use and on which the programme is dependent. Any item that will be operated for 10 000 hours and more should be purchased new. Second-hand plant or plant already company-owned is acceptable for support roles.

A decision has to be made on the disposal of each item of plant.

- Will it be kept by the company?
- Where will it be sent?
- Will it be sold locally?
- Will it be sold in an international auction?
- What is it likely to realize on disposal?
- Is there a guaranteed buyback from the supplier?

Shipping and inland transport

The procedure for shipping plant is the same as for materials, and is as discussed in chapter 9.

If there are no facilities for hire in the territory and the company has to provide vehicles to transport the plant from port to site, arrangements should be made for the plant and transport that is to be used in port clearance and inland transport to be sent separately in advance of the main deliveries.

Modern roll-on/roll-off vessels can take most of the plant for a large project as a single shipment. This is the cheapest method, but it has its risks. The Author has had the experience of a case when this method went badly wrong.

As the transport was needed first on arrival at the destination, it was organized to be put on the vessel last. However, when it came to loading the transport the captain of the vessel decided that it was already fully laden, and no amount of persuasion would make him change his mind. The vessel sailed without the transport, which then arrived six weeks later.

A similar method of shipping plant had been extremely successful on a previous project.

Maintenance and spares

If the plant is to operate over a long period of time, in arduous conditions, a strict policy of routine maintenance must be enforced.

The availability of spare parts is vital to maintaining production on site in a developing country. A fine judgement has to be made between on the one hand overprovision of spares and having to write off large costs at the end of the project, and on the other hand of running the risk of having plant broken down for longer than necessary, or needing a major airlift of spare parts. Delivery of spares may take three months, except if sent by air, and then the actual time taken is unpredictable, so the 'just in time' principle is inappropriate for a primitive location.

In some Third World territories, such as the Middle East, spares may be as readily available as at home. There the judgement of back-up availability should have been made in plant selection.

Earthmoving plant used for around 15 000 hours with extensive double-shifting over a four-year period, even with care and maintenance as good as is available in a developing country, may use spares which cost 125% of the capital cost of the plant for excavating plant and up to 150% for haulage plant. On a large project, spare parts can cost over £10 million a year, and involve the storage and handling of more than 10 000 items of stock.

The procedure for purchasing and shipping plant spares should be the same as for materials (chapter 9).

Initiation of purchases is done by the project office through the support office for offshore supply, and direct by the project office for onshore supply.

Spares holdings

When the plant is delivered to site, it should be accompanied by an initial spares holding. Ideally this spares holding should be established from company experience and records. Failing this, plant suppliers should provide recommendations for the initial amount.

Care should be taken to avoid the risk of the supplier taking the opportunity to sell slow-moving stock. If the supplier's advice is taken, it should be accompanied by a supplier's buyback agreement for stock left at the end of the contract. This initial holding should be sufficient for a minimum of three months' and a maximum of six months' plant usage.

Spares are to cover routine maintenance and breakdown. The storekeeping systems should be the same for spare parts as for materials. On a large civil engineering project, the number of plant spares in stock could be more than five times the number of construction items kept.

Maximum–minimum procedures for reordering spares should be the same as for materials (chapter 9), but for spares the project plant department must run a continuous audit on levels. The levels should be adjusted in accordance with the plant programme, so that as machines are demobilized stocks are reduced.

Spares used in repairs caused by accidents or in respect of claims under warranty should be recorded separately. Where the spares are specially purchased for these uses, the indents should be referenced with the occurrence, and reports should be attached. The more normal situation is that the spares will be taken from stock and should be coded and allocated against the occurrence.

The warranty and insurance procedure should be followed so that claims can be made as soon as possible and any inspections required by the suppliers or loss-adjusters can take place. The

```
┌─────────────────────────────────────────────────────────────────┐
│                        WARRANTY CLAIM                             │
│                                                                   │
│                           No ..................................   │
│  Site ...............................   Date ...................  │
│                                                                   │
│  Machine type .....................   Number .................   │
│  Engine type ......................   Number .................   │
│  Chassis type .....................   Number .................   │
│  Registration No. .................   Unit number                │
│  Miles/kilometres .................                               │
│  Machine hours ....................   Last filter change at ...  │
│  Oil pressure .....................   Grade oil used ..........   │
│  Time of Breakdown ................                               │
│  Approx. temperature ..............                               │
│  Last complete service ............   at............ h ....miles/km│
│  Field report: describe the failure                              │
│                                                                   │
│  What in your opinion caused failure?                            │
└─────────────────────────────────────────────────────────────────┘
```

Fig. 27. Warranty claim form

information likely to be required in a warranty claim is shown in Fig. 27.

Dependence on air freight must be minimized by good stock control and maintenance procedures.

Maintenance

Maintenance procedures should be set by the company's plant department. These should be tailored to the anticipated working conditions and the level of operator skill and competence.

The level of expatriate staff from the home base should depend on local capability and the degree of mechanization. A high level of European maintenance staff is normally advisable at the beginning of a plant-intensive civil engineering project. This should be reduced as the training programme improves local skills. Reduction from 50% European staff to 10−20% after the first year is a reasonable target.

The workshop and maintenance plant level should be set by the company's plant department. The general layout of a workshop for a large project is shown in Fig. 28, and a sample of the minimum tools and equipment in Table 9.

The purchase of fuel and lubricants and their use should be

controlled in accordance with the same procedure as for materials (chapter 9).

Asset management

When plant arrives on site, it should be listed in an asset register. This should record

- description of item

- anticipated life in hours

- cost, including freight

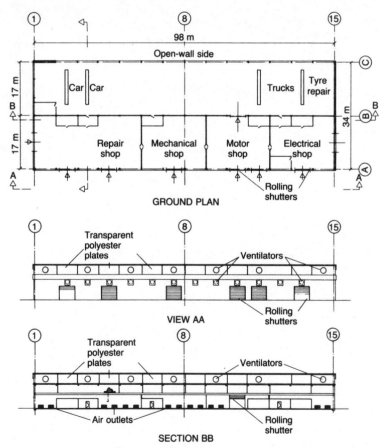

Fig. 28. (above and facing page). Workshop layout for a warm climate

- date of purchase
- major overhaul cost
- date of overhaul
- use to date in hours
- depreciation
- current book value
- anticipated resale value.

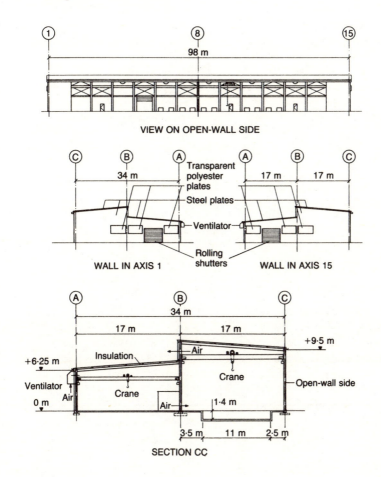

VIEW ON OPEN-WALL SIDE

WALL IN AXIS 1

WALL IN AXIS 15

SECTION CC

Table 9. Sample of workshop tools and equipment

Main equipment
Fitter's bench 2 m
6 in steel vice
Bench grinder 8 in
Bench drill stand
Compressor 14.5 ft³/min 110 V
5 kVA 1 pH 50 Hz 110 V
   generator
Electric welding set 200 A
Electric welding accessory kit
Battery charger/booster
Electric drill 110 V
Electric angle grinder 110 V
Electric 9 in hand circular saw
   110 V
Oxy-acetylene welding and
   cutting equipment with
   trolley and accessories
Storage racks
Tool chests and racks
Portable standard lamp
Hand leads and lights
Degrease bath
Rotary hand pumps for 205
   litre drums

Tools and accessories
Grinding wheel fine 25667
Grinding wheels coarse 24666
Tyre inflater PCL 5086
Tyre pressure gauge
   commercial
Blow guns
Air line and miscellaneous
   fittings
Twist drills set $\frac{1}{16} - \frac{1}{2}$ in by
   64ths

Twist drill parallel shank $\frac{9}{10}$ in
Twist drill parallel shank $\frac{5}{8}$ in
Cut-off wheels metal
Cut-off wheels stone
Rip and cross cut TC tipped
   blades 24314
Jerricans 20 litres (fuel)
Jerricans 20 litres (water)
$\frac{1}{2}$ in sq. drive mechanics tool
   kits NF 1 42K (fitters)
$\frac{3}{4}$ in sq. drive socket set NA
   467D
$\frac{1}{4}$ in sq. drive socket
   supplementary kit NA 349B
   metric
O/J spanners metric NB 351G
Ring spanners metric NC 389N
$\frac{1}{2}$ in sq. drive stud extractor
Stud extractor (easy out)
Torque wrench EVT 600A
Torque wrench EVT 3000A
Brake adjusters B216
Tool boxes similar B556
Padlocks and keys CEKA
   65/30
Padlocks and keys security
Hacksaw blades 12 in 24TPI
Files 6 in half-round smooth
Files 8 in HSF bastard
Files 10 in half-round 2nd cut
Files 12 in half-round bastard
Files 6 in round second cut
Files 10 in round bastard
Files handles
Mole grips 10 in
10 fT tapes P3ME
Mini-hacksaws

continued on facing page

Table 9 — continued

Mini-blades per 100
Magneto spanner sets NB 108T
Adjustable spanners 8 in auto
Adjustable spanners 15 in
Stillson wrenches 8 in
Stillson 36 in 300/36
Wire brushes 4-row
Oil cans (squirt 1 pt)
Drain plug spanners
Valve grinding sockets
Tester screwdrivers 12/24 V
Pin punch set
Oil measures 1 gall
Oil measures $\frac{1}{2}$ gall
Oil measures 1 pt
Oil funnels
Fuel funnels
Safety goggles
Welding goggles lens plain 2 in dia.
Welding goggles lens coloured 2 in dia.
Welding goggles lens plain 4.25 in × 3.25 in
Welding goggles lens coloured 4.25 in × 3.25 in
Sykes puller kit 186504
Commercial tyre levers
Axle stands model AS20
Axle stands model AS30
Hydraulic jack 5 tons
Hydraulic trolley jack 2 t
Hydraulic trolley jack 1.5 t
Spider wheel brace car
Spider wheel brace commercial
Volume buckets grease
Volume buckets oil

Thread files 015600 BSF and white
Thread files 015601 AN
Thread files 015602 HH
Thread files 015603 BSP
Ring punch kit (Maby)
Pipe flaring kit
Record bolt croppers 30 in
Record bolt cropper blades
Hand chain block (3 T 3 m) EQS
Chain pullers (1.75 t × 1.5 m) EWS
Carpenter's basic tool kit
Sledge-hammer 14 lb
Wrecking bar 36 in
Nail-puller
Crowbar 5 ft
Spirit level 1 m
Blowlamp (LPG)
Blowlamp cylinders (local)
Soldering iron 8 oz
Electrical soldering iron medium S140
Valve spring compressors
Bush punch kit
Circlip pliers external
Circlip pliers internal
Tinsnips straight 10 in
Tinsnips curved 10 in
Hand valve seat refacer
Universal clutch spiggot tool
Wad punches
Loctite O ring kit Imperial
Loctite O ring kit metric
Windscreen tools
Hydrometer

continued overleaf

Table 9 — continued

Hydraulic Discharge Tester

Distilled water

Battery jump cables

Avo meter

Ripaults crompers access

Workshop kit cold vulcanize

Radial repair units

Schrader valve tools

Lazy tongs (pop rivet)

Paint brushes 1 in

Paint brushes $1\frac{1}{2}$ in

Paint brushes 3 in

Grease guns

Trimming knives

G cramps 6 in

Consumables

Miltrode electrodes

Miltrode 3.25 mm × 450 mm
    long cartons

Miltrode 4 mm × 450 mm
    long cartons

Weartrodes 3.25 mm

SIF bronze 12.4 mm

SIF steel No. 11 1.2 mm

SIF steel No. 11 2.0 mm

SIF steel No. 11 3.2 mm

SIF Flux SIF bronze 450 g

Bakers fluid

Cored solder reels

Tinmans solder stocks

Screws $\frac{7}{16}$ in × $2\frac{1}{2}$ in UNC HT

Screws $\frac{1}{2}$ in × 3 in UNF HY

Screws $\frac{1}{4}$ in × 3 in UNC HT

Screws 12 mm × 75 mm

metric HT bolts

Screws $\frac{1}{2}$ in × 3 in BSF HT

Screws $\frac{1}{2}$ in × $2\frac{1}{2}$ in UNF HT

Screws $\frac{1}{2}$ in × $2\frac{1}{2}$ in UNC HT

6 mm metric nuts

$\frac{1}{4}$ in BSF nuts

$\frac{1}{4}$ in NUF nuts

$\frac{3}{4}$ in UNC nuts

$\frac{1}{4}$ in flat washers

$\frac{1}{4}$ in spring washers

8 mm metric nuts

$\frac{5}{16}$ in BSF nuts

$\frac{5}{16}$ in UNF nuts

$\frac{5}{16}$ in UNC nuts

$\frac{5}{16}$ in flat washers

$\frac{5}{16}$ in spring washers

10 mm metric nuts

$\frac{3}{8}$ in BSF nuts

$\frac{3}{8}$ in UNF nuts

$\frac{3}{8}$ in NUC nuts

$\frac{3}{8}$ in flat washers

$\frac{3}{8}$ in spring washers

$\frac{7}{16}$ in BSF nuts

$\frac{7}{16}$ in UNF nuts

$\frac{7}{16}$ in UNC nuts

$\frac{7}{16}$ in flat washers

$\frac{7}{16}$ in spring washers

12 mm metric nuts

$\frac{1}{2}$ in BSF nuts

$\frac{1}{2}$ in UNF nuts

$\frac{1}{2}$ in UNC nuts

$\frac{1}{2}$ in flat washers

$\frac{1}{2}$ in spring washers

Assorted split pins 3 mm

Assorted self-tapping screws 6 mm

---

continued on facing page

Table 9 — continued

Assorted spire nuts 8 mm
Assorted copper washers 11 mm
Assorted fibre washers 19 mm
Assorted clevis pins 36 mm
Assorted pop rivets
Hermetite red
Hermetite green
Boss white jointing
Thread tape PTFE
Crocodile clips 25 amp
Electric cable single (cars) 14.012
Electric cable twin (cars) 14.012
Battery cable light duty 5 m
Battery cable heavy duty 5 m
Battery terminals (positive) B32
Battery terminals (negative) B33
Emery cloth fine 1 in × 180 grit
Emery cloth medium 1 in × 100 grit
Emery cloth coarse 1 in × 60 grit
Jenolite (erasing oil) 1 pt
Hand cleanser Swarfega
Grinding paste fine and coarse 277
Copper locking wire 18 g
Copper tube $\frac{3}{16}$ in NB
Copper tube $\frac{1}{4}$ in NB
Copper tube $\frac{5}{16}$ in NB
Plastic nylon tubing $\frac{3}{16}$ in NB

Plastic nylon tubing $\frac{1}{4}$ in NB
Plastic nylon tubing $\frac{5}{16}$ in NB
Plastic nylon tubing $\frac{3}{8}$ in NB
Plastic nylon tubing $\frac{1}{4}$ in NB
Ferrules etc. $\frac{3}{16}$ in
Ferrules etc. $\frac{1}{4}$ in
Ferrules etc. $\frac{5}{16}$
Ferrules etc. $\frac{3}{8}$ in
Ferrules etc. $\frac{1}{2}$ in
$\frac{1}{2}$ in NB heater hose
$\frac{3}{4}$ in NB heater hose
1 in heater hose
Assorted compression springs CS 172
Assorted tension springs ES 171
Assorted grease nipples 124M
Air hose
1 in dia. Jubilee clips 1A
2 in dia. Jubilee clips 2X
3 in dia. Jubilee clips 4
4 in dia. Jubilee clips 5
5 amp fuse wire 100 g
10 amp fuse wire 100 g
15 amp fuse wire 100 g
20 amp fuse wire 100 g
25 amp fuse wire 100 g
Insulating tape 1 in
Mo cloths
Gasket material $\frac{1}{32}$ in
Gasket material $\frac{1}{16}$ in
Nylon rope (lifting stops)
Nails and screws (carpenter's section)

At six-monthly intervals, the information in the asset register for individual items of plant should be used in setting charge-out rates in the project costing system. It is important that this updating takes place to avoid an unrealistically high book value for plant being left on completion of its use for the project.

The asset register should be subjected to a technical audit at six-monthly intervals to ensure that the anticipated remaining life of the plant is realizable without unscheduled major overhauls.

Disposal

The disposal of plant may take place locally or may be through an international auction at a central location in the region. Singapore, for instance, has major plant auctions from time to time.

Disposal locally may not be possible due to duty-free import into the territory, which requires re-export. Bonds may have been given as assurance for this when the plant was initially imported. Furthermore, the duty that may be levied in the event of the plant being retained in the territory for local sale may be based on the original imported value, including freight.

The duty-free import of spares can cause complications. In some countries, the parts that have been replaced have to be made available for re-export. The procedure for dealing with spares on a duty-free contract must be clearly established at the beginning.

The company may wish to keep some plant for use on other projects. This may not be permitted if the plant is for use in the same territory and it was imported duty-free, and these other projects do not have duty-free status.

As a major company asset is involved, plant disposal (like plant purchase) should be subject to senior company approval.

11 Security and crisis management

Security includes the prevention of threats to

- people
- assets
- funds.

Security has become, if anything, an even greater matter of concern than before. The personal security of staff and the prevention of theft have always been important in the developing world. Recent events in the Middle East have demonstrated the need to have a well thought out plan for dealing with crises that can be implemented as soon as the events occur.

Getting European staff to work in developing countries in the future will be extremely difficult. Not only will prospects within the developed economies offer attractive sources of employment but the risks in the Third World will assume a high profile. Effective planning for security and crisis management have therefore become important for recruiting good expatriate staff.

External threats such as war and invasion and internal crime, insecurity and guerrilla activity are common occurrences. Some aspects can be covered by insurance, but the protection of personnel and assets are the prime responsibility of management. Management must seek to develop in all employees a constant and instinctive awareness of security considerations by means of

- personal example
- informing staff of their obligations
- regular monitoring of security practice.

Figure 29 shows the pattern of security thinking on a large

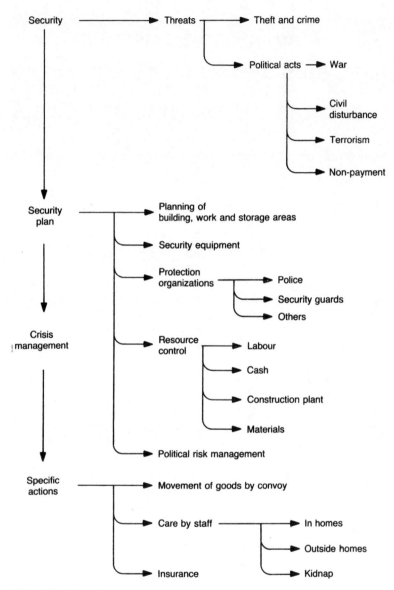

Fig. 29. Security pattern

project. As shown, security also includes measures to manage the financial exposure caused by non-payment due to a political act or simple lack of funds.

Security is analysed in this chapter under the following headings

- threats to security
- security plan
- crisis management
- vehicle convoys
- care by staff in respect of own security.

Threats to security

The threats to security will increase as work expands due to the following

- importation of non-regional (often rootless) labour into the area and the problems posed by discarded labour of this type who remain in the area
- increase in the value of attractive goods at site
- increase in the overall wealth in the area.

The basic threats to security are crime and political acts.

Crime

Types of crime include

- theft off-site (e.g. at docks, airports, warehouses)
- theft by employees (including servants)
- theft by outsiders (and common local criminals)
- fraud and corruption
- vandalism
- extortion
- other common criminal activity.

Targets for crime are

- cash (including cheques, air tickets, etc.)

- motor vehicles and small items of plant
- tools
- small spares for plant (particularly for cars)
- timber and other bulk stores, including fuel
- consumable stores and protective clothing
- foodstuffs
- explosives
- personal effects (including passports)
- information and records.

Locations for crime include

- plant stores and workshops
- main stores (all types)
- wages office and main office
- mess and canteens
- domestic housing.

Political acts

War presents a direct threat to personnel and goods, whether it is in the territory of the project or in territories that lie on the communication routes. Very few major construction companies have avoided being in territories where war has broken out.

Somewhat more prevalent than war are civil disturbances, which are endemic in the Third World. The vast differences between the haves and the have nots make these actions inevitable.

In many countries, civil disturbance takes the more covert route of acts of terrorism. These can be directed against high-profile construction projects, or can occur in the privileged areas where expatriates take their leisure.

War, civil disturbance and terrorism should all feature in the security planning which is now discussed.

A non-payment risk may also arise due to political acts or lack of funds. This lack of funds may be due to economic deterioration of the country, or Client difficulties. In most developing countries security planning must provide measures to minimize exposure to this risk.

The security plan
The security plan should involve

- planning the location and layout of buildings, and work and storage areas
- selection of security equipment
- involvement of organizations that can provide some aspect of protection
- the control of resources, including security procedures
- exposure control in respect of non-payment or termination.

Planning of the location, layout and details of buildings and areas
   Site layout. Aspects of site layout to be considered are

- access to controlled areas of site and camp
- need for gatehouse(s)
- security fencing and lighting
- siting of buildings, especially those of a sensitive nature, such as high-value stores, food and drink stores, where cash is kept at a counter, etc.
- location of site stores and storage areas, particularly fuels, explosives etc.
- location of plant and vehicle parks.

Location and layout of buildings. Offices and stores areas should be located near the main gate, so that visitors, suppliers and other third parties have only a short distance to cover to reach them, and there is only a small area to which they have easy access in doing so.

Buildings and stores subject to the greatest security risk (such as wages office, plant stores and workshops) should be sited well away from the perimeter fence.

A sterile area should be kept clear inside and outside the

perimeter fence to discourage small items being thrown over the fence and collected later.

Buildings should be so sited that entrances to 'sensitive' areas are not shielded from view by security personnel or employees at their normal place of work, and so can be easily overlooked.

Building protection. Be guided by precautions taken by others in similar situations. Take serious note of measures recommended by the local police.

Examine all buildings from the outside, keeping in mind information gained on the usual methods of entry by local thieves. Regard any aperture more than 0.05 m^2 (including windows merely glazed) as a potential risk.

Consider locks, bolts, bars and grilles — but retain a sense of proportion!

Assume that intruders will usually be put off if faced with a fair amount of noisy or time-consuming work. Intrusion is usually effected through doors and windows — often with the aid of tools found on location.

Provided the structure is adequate, intruders are usually effectively deterred by

- doors: 50 mm softwood with solid panels, fitted with good quality lock and hinge bolts; for residences, a spyhole and a chain on the door give extra security; provide inside bolts (top and bottom) to all other doors, particularly those to which a servant has a key

- shutters: not less than 25 mm thick timber of 13 mm ply; existing shutters below standard can be reinforced with min. 16 gauge sheet steel

- wire grilles: not less than 8 gauge

- iron bars: 16 mm dia. at not less than 125 mm centres.

All shutters, grilles and bars must be securely fixed to the main structure in such a way that they cannot be unscrewed or dislodged from the outside. Locks should be of good quality.

Locking-up routines are essential, in residences, stores and offices. Clear standing instructions on locking must be given regularly to staff and servants.

In certain situations, such as isolated dwellings and particularly valuable stores, intruder alarms or other electronic devices may be desirable. Contact the company security officer for detailed recommendations and advice.

The erection of a security fence will help to deter casual entry, but may not stop a determined thief. Trees and bushes should be cleared immediately inside the fence to provide a sterile area.

If possible, the sterile area should be lit, but avoid glare shining directly into bedroom windows.

A more secure arrangement is to erect a second fence about 1 m inside the main fence and lay coiled barbed wire between.

All fences should be inspected daily and any attempted breaches reported and repaired immediately.

Isolated dwellings. The protection of isolated dwellings outside camp areas may need special consideration. Detailed attention to residence security, coupled with 'good neighbour' schemes should generally be adequate, but the use of intruder alarms, sirens or citizens' band radios, may also be desirable. Individual night-watchmen, even if not wholly reliable, should give added comfort. The section on residence security, under 'Care by staff in respect of own security' later in this chapter, describes security procedure for these circumstances in more detail.

Security alarms

There is a large range of security alarm equipment on the market. The security plan must identify its appropriateness to the territory and to the type of security risk.

Before a decision is made on any intruder alarm, the following should be determined.

- *Cost.* In a simple system, much of the cost is incurred in the installation of the hard wiring.

- *Response.* What action will be generated by the alarm sounding?

- *Installation.* Advanced types need expert installation and maintenance. Site electricians are usually capable of handling basic systems provided that they have received some training and instruction. (A suitable site electrician can be sent on a short course dealing with the installation of a simple intruder alarm. Such courses are held in the UK by major companies. The group security officer can advise.)

- *Back-up.* In the less developed territories, consideration must be given to the availability of back-up facilities and resources to deal with the inevitable malfunction and fault-finding.

A survey should be carried out to determine the following.

- *Suitability of premises.* An intruder alarm should not be used in premises which are dilapidated or badly constructed. Additional protection in these circumstances is illusory and the structural defects constitute a potential source of false alarms.

- *Environmental suitability.* Continuous steam, excessive heat or cold, moisture, water, acid fumes, chemicals, forced-air heating, birds and many other similar factors can have an adverse effect on equipment and cause false alarms.

- *Nature of contents.* Are any of the contents particularly attractive to thieves? Are the attractive contents dispersed throughout the premises? Is it possible to concentrate the attractive goods into one area which can be isolated, thus reducing the total area to be protected?

- *The likelihood of collusion.* Will employees forget to switch the system on?

Installation of the equipment is as follows.

- Magnetic contacts are fitted to external doors, windows and cupboards.

- Pressure mats made of plastic are fitted beneath floor-coverings.

- Windows are fitted with magnetic contacts if they are suitable. Where shutters have been fitted, it is usually better to fit the contacts to the shutters.

- Infra-red person detectors are fitted.

- Magnetic contacts are fitted to trapdoors giving access to roof voids.

- Personal-attack switches are fitted adjacent to beds and within easy reach of the door from which callers can be seen.

- The control box is installed in a cupboard or recess out of sight.

- The bell/siren is fitted in a prominent position on the outside of the building, out of reach.

The above system should activate an alarm if intrusion is attempted via external doors, windows or trapdoors. It can also be activated by the occupants if there are troublesome callers or if prowlers are spotted outside at night. Personal-attack alarms are always in circuit and should operate at any time.

Sometimes it is not possible to fit contacts to windows. If so, it will be necessary to supplement the system by fitting contacts to internal doors and placing pressure mats in strategic places. Remember that pressure mats can be actuated by the weight of an average-sized dog.

Organizations which provide protection
Police. It is essential that the co-operation of the local police is obtained, even if the part they play in day-to-day security is limited. At the least they will

- provide information on known criminals

- investigate incidents

- prosecute offenders through the courts

- remove/lock up serious offenders when required.

Early contact should be made, preferably through the most senior officer at the appropriate headquarters. If possible, an introduction should be obtained from the highest (e.g. ministerial) level.

The objectives are

- to obtain the co-operation of the local force

- to explain the company's operations and the effect on the local crime picture

- to establish routine communication links

- to identify and initiate the practical help which the police can provide

- to discuss the desirability of establishing a sub-police post in or near site; it may be worthwhile for the Company to provide a suitable building and compound

- to obtain information on the past and possible future incidence and types of crime in the area, and on the identification of known criminals in the area

- to obtain advice on security.

Special consultation with the police should precede the storage of explosives or hazardous materials.

An assessment of the competence of the local police is probably best derived from discussions with officials of the UK embassy or high commission and selected managers or senior officials of local organizations.

It should be remembered that the attitudes of the local police are almost invariably those of the populace at large or of the group in power. Even a hint of disapproval can cause much harm to future relations. It is better to recognize and use the good qualities of the police rather than to become deterred by those aspects of behaviour that expatriates do not understand or approve. Criticism should be avoided or kept to the most private of circumstances and never expressed in correspondence as it is certain that the police will become aware of it.

Company's own security guards organization. Responsibility for routine security matters should be delegated by the Project Manager to a senior member of the staff, to be security manager as an additional responsibility over and above his normal function. This individual must have direct access to the Project Manager, and his duties should permit him to visit any part of the site, offices or stores at any time and for any reason. Ideally he will have normal daily contact with both senior and junior staff and supervisors.

His duties must be confirmed in writing. In addition to a roving commission, they should include

- personal investigation of all serious lapses of security

- advising the Project Manager of security weaknesses

- regular inspection of security measures and equipment

- responsibility for the performance of the security force.

The security force should normally be under the control of a locally employed chief security officer, who will often be a former military or police sergeant or sergeant-major. His main tasks will be to prevent crime on site and to protect company goods. As security is a 24-hour business, the appointment of a deputy is usually desirable to assist in effective supervision of the force.

The Chief Security Officer should be empowered to discharge and immediately remove from site any security employee found drunk or sleeping on duty. A security employee suspected or accused of corruption or other misdemeanour should be referred to the Security Manager.

Usually a head security guard should be responsible for each shift in each security zone.

Guards operating in random patrols, possibly accompanied by dogs, are usually more effective than static watchmen (who are nevertheless required in some situations). Patrols should vary their routes, but be instructed to clock in or report at about two-hourly intervals.

Static and night watchmen should be provided with some shelter from the elements which does not prevent them from observing movement in the vicinity. Guards are not usually armed, but should be given a weapon for self-defence (such as a stout stick, pick helve or panga), which will also give them more confidence in challenging intruders. They should be equipped with a torch (but ration and mark all batteries) and a whistle. A distinctive uniform should be provided, including a safety helmet of different colour from those of the workforce.

Careful selection of security personnel is essential and should always be vetted by the local police. It is generally advisable to recruit security personnel from a different area or tribe from that of the majority of the workforce, but avoiding extreme ethnic differences. Beware of local family ties.

Security standing orders should include clear instructions to security employees on the types of incident to be reported, whether they should be reported immediately or at end of shift, and to whom.

A daybook should be maintained by the Chief Security Officer in which all incidents, unusual occurrences or suspicious circumstances are recorded. This book should be inspected regularly by the Security Manager.

Any items of importance should be advised to the Project Manager on a standard incident report form as shown in Fig. 30.

Others. Contact should be made with the nearest embassy (or

141

high commission or consulate) to obtain general information on the locality, arrange for the registration of future UK site staff and families, and agree contacts and communication methods in the event of an emergency.

Discussion with representatives of other (particularly foreign) organizations working in the area can give an indication of the most prevalent types of crime (and techniques) common to the area.

As for private security organizations, be wary of

INCIDENT REPORT FORM

Contract No.

Contract

To

Nature of occurrence

Section or location

Date and time of incident

Reported to (A)   Name

By   Name

Witnesses   Name

(add further names   Name

and addresses if

necessary on

reverse)

Details of incident

Action taken by (A)

(Estimated order of cost

to rectify)

Date   Signed (A)

Remarks

Office use

Claim No.

Date

Time

Note. Add additional details and/or sketch as appropriate on back.

Signed

Fig. 30

- big names — the local organization will only be as good as its local representative

- official recommendations — because of the possibility of commission payments.

One aspect of security is the protection offered by insurance companies. This is reduced by the size of excess amounts which apply to the policies. The level of excesses and the premium costs, or indeed the availability of insurance in some cases, are affected by the insurer's perception of the quality of the site security in force and the claims record.

Control of resources and security procedures

Labour: recruitment and control. Check recruitment procedures and ensure a controlled flow of applicants from gate to interview, trade testing, starting procedure etc.

It is usually necessary to set up a reporting centre off-site for applicants where they can be mustered and controlled (especially if a main gate does not yet exist). The issue of temporary identification may be desirable on large sites where applicants may become lost.

Security vetting procedures should be established, especially for staff in 'sensitive' appointments. Procedures include checking with previous employers, police and independent referees. (Fidelity bonding is seldom practical in most overseas locations.)

Following engagement, it is desirable that each employee is issued with some form of identification with a passport type photograph attached.

Labour: gatehouse and search procedures. Whether or not regular personal search procedures are applied, barriers should be erected at gates to funnel all pedestrians leaving the site under the watchful eye of a security officer.

A metal, counterbalanced pole barrier is recommended to control vehicle access by day. Gates may be provided for additional security at night.

Adequate parking areas should be ensured both outside and inside gates.

The gatehouse should be connected to the main office by telephone.

Search procedures, even if random, should apply to all

nationalities. Hand-held metal-detectors for body-scanning may be useful. The group security officer should provide details of these and other detection equipment.

Local employees transported by bus to and from site should be debussed and embussed outside the main gate.

Loiterers should be discouraged outside the main gate. Special arrangements should be made for the control of applicants for employment.

Labour: discharge for theft. Be extremely chary of retaining any employee caught stealing, for example on the grounds that he is a first-class worker and cannot be replaced. The chances that he has only stolen on this one occasion and will never do so again, given the opportunity, are remote. (It may be only the first time he has been caught.)

Maintain a register (with photograph if possible) of all employees caught stealing as they may apply again for employment, possibly using a different name.

Bear in mind that usually the great bulk of theft (especially of smaller items) is carried out by employees and not outsiders.

Servants. The principles for employing personal and domestic servants should be established. It is usually desirable that they go through the normal company recruitment process (including medical check), that a register of names is maintained, and that they too are issued with identification tags (or whatever system is being used).

Plant. Theft of major items of plant is relatively rare, but attractive components (e.g. batteries) will often be stolen when plant is left unattended. There is also the danger of vandalism where plant is left unattended in remote places. When possible, mobile plant should be parked up in areas where surveillance can be organized, and static plant should be anchored down.

Vehicles are more often and more easily stolen. All cars should be fitted with steering locks or other security devices appropriate to the conditions. Standing instructions should be given to all drivers and staff regarding the dangers of leaving vehicles unattended.

Fuel and lubricant stores must be secure, no-smoking areas. Early attention must be given to the proper recording on signature of issues of fuel for plant and vehicles (see under 'Storage and issue' in chapter 9).

Particular care must be taken of

- overnight security of mobile plant and vehicles
o immobilization
o control of keys

- fuel storage and issue checks.

Materials. Establish initial adequately secure start-up storage facilities and simple materials-received and materials-issue procedures. Initiate a system for requisitions for the issue of

- security equipment

- fencing and lighting

- watchmen's and security guards' equipment

- safes

- cash and wage boxes for transportation.

Cash: general. Arrangements are required as follows.

- Determine the maximum amounts of cash to be held at each cash point.

- Select suitable fireproof safes.

- Establish cash-control procedures including collection of wages and how carried.

- Arrange insurance of cash on site and in transit.

- Arrange insurance of personal effects (and brief arriving staff on it).

Safes and document storage. The following considerations apply.

- *Cash.* Establish requirements for safes (size, type and value of contents) for
o cashier's office
o main office(s)
o mess and canteens
o club etc.

- *Documents.* Organize secure storage in fireproof cabinets, safes and the like for

o tender documents and make-up of prices
o contract documents
o accounts ledgers
o cash-books
o passports
o other important documents

● *Other.* Valuables needing secure storage are
o keys
o cheque books
o air tickets etc.

Note that copies of original correspondence, drawings, staff records, payrolls, accounts and tax information etc. not retained in fireproof safes should be kept in a separate location in case the originals are destroyed by fire.

Cash floats. Petty cash floats at camp, in canteens etc. should be held only with the Project Manager's approval. All amounts held must be kept in a secure cash-box in a locked drawer or cabinet or, if in excess of approximately £100, in a proper safe.

Floats should be physically checked at least monthly by the Project Manager or the senior accountant personally.

All withdrawals from a cash float must be entered daily in a cash-book, kept separately.

Transportation of cash. Where large sums of cash have to be transported by road, the following should be noted

● Consideration should be given to local experience and proved countermeasures against theft.

● Transportation of cash in excess of about £1000 should involve at least two responsible staff members working together.

● If the amount is in excess of about £5000, a second vehicle should always accompany the vehicle which is carrying the cash.

● The use of armed police escorts is not always desirable, but this depends on the territory and the distances involved.

● In many developing countries, guard dogs may be a more effective deterrent than firearms, and present less of a security risk.

- Times of collection and routes should be varied as much as possible.

- An internationally recognized cash-carrying company should be used, if available.

Overnight storage of cash on site. Overnight storage of cash on site is to be avoided if at all possible. It may be possible to make up wage packets on bank premises or return made-up packets to a bank overnight (provided that small banks in remote areas are sufficiently secure).

If overnight storage on site is unavoidable, the insurance requirements should be checked. If insurance cover is impractical or too expensive, the Project Manager must use his own discretion regarding the advisability of using police or local guards. Large amounts of cash must not be left unguarded in site offices, even in safes. It may be preferable and more secure if the money is held in camp by expatriate staff, possibly in smaller-value lots.

Wages office. Especially when used for making up pay packets, the wages office should be located in such a position that access is restricted and that the building is adjacent to other buildings containing a number of trustworthy employees, such as the main office block.

The building must be of solid construction, having windows which permit good visibility from the inside outwards but not the reverse.

The building and doors should be built to a standard sufficient to resist a sledge-hammer attack for about ten minutes.

The use of alarm facilities and personal-attack buttons should be considered.

Local experience should be used as a guide.

Risk of non-payment and termination

There is a risk that a project may be terminated for various reasons, including political acts. Also, due to lack of Client funds, non-payment may occur. Whatever rights there may be under the contract are illusory if a Client is unable pay.

In long-duration contracts, initially credit-worthy clients may run out of funds. It is therefore necessary for a continuous risk-exposure analysis to be included among the security measures.

The principal risks are as follows.

- Payment may stop but expenditure and commitments continue.
- Investment in plant may not be realizable, or at worst plant may be confiscated.
- It may be impossible to make an immediate stop to the flow of imported materials.
- Expatriates will have to be retained or repatriated.

Table 10 (below and facing page). Exposure calculation

Based on contract cash flow as shown in columns A (month in) and B (month out), written-down value (WDV) as shown in column E and termination four months after expenditure from last payment — reflected in column G, further commitments are additional costs are additional costs at the fourth month after last payment — reflected in column J

Month from contract signature	Cash		Other factors			Cash exposure				
	A	B	C	D	E	F	G	H	I	Total
1	9823	3536	400	100	2500	6287	(6796)	(800)	(100)	(1409)
2	262	988	600	100	2450	5561	(7789)	(800)	(100)	(3128)
3	2016	1587	800	100	2400	5990	(8016)	(800)	(100)	(2926)
4	1292	1656	800	100	2350	5626	(8265)	(1000)	(100)	(3739)
5	1164	2565	800	100	2300	4225	(7455)	(1000)	(100)	(4330)
6	1009	1981	800	100	2250	3253	(7679)	(1000)	(100)	(5526)
7	1187	1814	800	100	2200	2626	(7906)	(1000)	(100)	(6380)
8	1297	1905	1000	100	2150	2018	(7655)	(1000)	(100)	(6737)
9	1558	1755	1000	100	2100	1821	(7610)	(1000)	(100)	(6889)
10	1672	2205	1000	100	2050	1288	(7189)	(1000)	(100)	(7001)
11	1577	2041	1000	100	2000	824	(7060)	(1000)	(100)	(7336)
12	1831	1654	1000	100	1950	1001	(7261)	(900)	(100)	(7260)
13	1852	1710	1000	100	1900	1143	(7297)	(900)	(100)	(7154)
14	1819	1784	1000	100	1850	1178	(7339)	(900)	(100)	(7161)
15	1818	1912	1000	100	1800	1084	(7149)	(700)	(100)	(6865)
16	2126	1855	900	100	1750	1355	(7000)	(700)	(100)	(6445)
17	2283	1746	900	100	1700	1892	(6659)	(500)	(100)	(5367)
18	2260	1826	900	100	1650	2326	(5953)	(500)	(100)	(4227)
19	2186	1722	700	100	1600	2790	(5017)	(500)	(100)	(2827)
20	1906	1706	700	100	1550	2990	(3982)	(300)	(100)	(1392)
21	1554	1405	500	100	1500	3139	(3024)	(200)	(100)	(185)
22	1338	1120	500	100	1450	3357	(2105)	(200)	(100)	952
23	1198	786	500	100	1400	3769	(1474)	(100)	(100)	2095
24	929	671	300	100	1350	4027	(958)	(100)	(100)	2869
25	601	447	200	100	1300	4181	(637)	(100)	(100)	3344
26	402	201	200	100	1250	4382	(524)	(100)	(100)	3658

The exposure analysis and plan should continuously show

- estimate of maximum exposure at various stages
- lay-off of risk through insurance or other provisions
- identification of early warnings and associated remedial actions.

A typical spread-sheet exposure calculation is shown in Table 10.

commitments as shown in column C, additional costs as shown in column D, plant any default and therefore assuming at any point future expense is four months' commitments at the fourth month after last payment — reflected in column H, further in column I, and plant residuals realized eight months after last payment — reflected

J	Cash exposure	Bonds					Plant exposure	Total exposure
		Advance	Plant	Perform	Reten-tion	Total		
2100	691	(9823)	—	(4911)	—	(14 734)	(2500)	(16 543)
2050	(1078)	(9753)	—	(4911)	—	(14 664)	(2450)	(18 192)
2000	(926)	(9216)	—	(4911)	—	(14 127)	(2400)	(17 453)
1950	(1789)	(8872)	—	(4911)	—	(13 783)	(2350)	(17 922)
1900	(2430)	(8562)	—	(4911)	—	(13 473)	(2300)	(18 203)
1850	(3676)	(8293)	—	(4911)	—	(13 204)	(2250)	(19 130)
1800	(4580)	(7977)	—	(4911)	—	(12 858)	(2200)	(19 668)
1750	(4987)	(7631)	—	(4911)	—	(12 542)	(2150)	(19 679)
1700	(5189)	(7215)	—	(4911)	—	(12 126)	(2100)	(19 415)
1650	(5351)	(6769)	—	(4911)	—	(11 680)	(2050)	(19 018)
1600	(5736)	(6348)	—	(4911)	—	(11 259)	(2000)	(18 995)
1550	(5710)	(5860)	—	(4911)	—	(10 771)	(1950)	(18 431)
1500	(5654)	(5366)	—	(4911)	—	(10 277)	(1900)	(17 831)
1450	(5711)	(4881)	—	(4911)	—	(9792)	(1850)	(17 308)
1400	(5465)	(4396)	—	(4911)	—	(9307)	(1800)	(16 572)
1350	(5095)	(3835)	—	(4911)	—	(8746)	(1750)	(15 591)
1300	(4067)	(3264)	—	(4911)	—	(8175)	(1700)	(13 942)
1250	(2977)	(2699)	—	(4911)	—	(7610)	(1650)	(12 237)
1200	(1627)	(2152)	—	(4911)	—	(7063)	(1600)	(10 290)
1150	(242)	(1675)	—	(4911)	—	(6586)	(1550)	(8378)
1100	915	(1286)	—	(4911)	—	(6197)	(1500)	(6782)
1050	2002	(951)	—	(4911)	—	(5862)	(1450)	(5310)
1000	3095	(652)	—	(4911)	—	(5563)	(1400)	(3868)
950	3819	(420)	—	(4911)	—	(5331)	(1350)	(2862)
900	4244	(270)	—	(4911)	—	(5181)	(1300)	(2237)
0	3658	(169)	—	(4911)	—	(5080)	(1250)	(2672)

Insurance may be available to cover the exposure, but this is likely to be costly. A compromise of some insurance and the recognition of the need for provision against the remaining exposure is a more likely answer.

Crisis management

Usually crises occur with little or no warning. During such crises, communications with the UK are usually (although not inevitably) broken. Consequently assistance from the home office cannot be expected.

It is therefore desirable that at an early stage in the new contract the project management prepares rudimentary but flexible 'contingency plans' which can be activated promptly in the case of an unforeseen emergency.

Broad details should be advised to the UK operations director so that in the event of a crisis the home office has some idea what the local management intend to do and how they might be contacted.

Commercial undertakings can deal efficiently with most problems provided that they use their traditional management skills rather than rely on intuitive or emotional responses.

Contingency planning

The first priority of the company's management in an emergency should be to safeguard the lives and persons of staff, their families and uninvolved labour. The second is to safeguard company property and reputation.

It is recommended that a small 'crisis management team' be set up early in the contract, reporting to the Project Manager (who may or may not be a member). A team of three is suggested, but other staff may be identified who can be co-opted at a later date.

Investigation and evaluation. The initial functions of the team should be

- to collect and analyse information in order to assess
- o the degree of domestic stability in the country
- o the possibility of conflict between the host country and another
- o the political climate and its influence on social and economic stability
- o the degrees of risk of terrorism, kidnapping, unrest and major criminal activity

- to make contact with the nearest British embassy, high commission or consulate and establish a procedure for the registration of all UK expatriate staff (if this has not already been done).

- to evaluate the likely effectiveness of communications with and arrangements by embassy/commission/consulate in an emergency.

Preparation of contingency plan. The team should then prepare an outline contingency plan for the approval of the Project Manager, giving consideration to

- individual duties and responsibilities in the event of emergency, including
- o communication with the embassy etc. and head office
- o promulgation of information to and communication with staff and labour
- o relocation of outlying staff in central area
- o central stocks of food, water and fuel
- o protection of families
- o medical
- o transport
- o repatriation arrangements
- o storage of personal effects in the event of mass repatriation
- o protection of company property, plant, equipment and stores (including fuel) and subsequent storage etc.
- o company documents
- o shutting down sections of work
- o what do do about local labour and staff

- composition of the full 'crisis management committee', which should probably be larger than the team, and should be led by the Project Manager in person; it is recommended that the committee include a suitably qualified woman, ideally one with nursing experience, to assist in looking after women and children

- the outline plan (which should be updated from time to time as necessary); it should be kept strictly confidential and issued only to members of the small crisis management team, the Project Manager and the UK operations director.

The crisis

If an outline contingency plan exists and the composition of the crisis management committee has been predetermined, it should be relatively easy to move without panic into a situation where the committee establishes firm control. Even so, there are likely to be problems which have not been foreseen and which have to

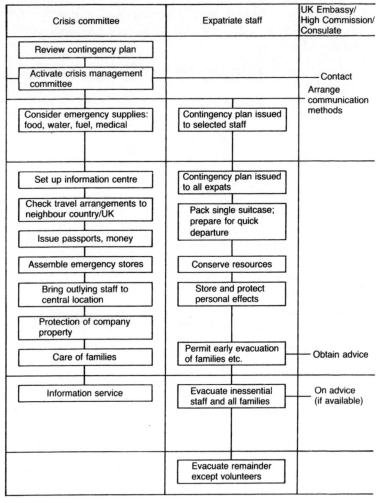

Crisis committee	Expatriate staff	UK Embassy/ High Commission/ Consulate
Review contingency plan		
Activate crisis management committee		Contact Arrange communication methods
Consider emergency supplies: food, water, fuel, medical	Contingency plan issued to selected staff	
Set up information centre	Contingency plan issued to all expats	
Check travel arrangements to neighbour country/UK	Pack single suitcase; prepare for quick departure	
Issue passports, money		
Assemble emergency stores	Conserve resources	
Bring outlying staff to central location	Store and protect personal effects	
Protection of company property		
Care of families	Permit early evacuation of families etc.	Obtain advice
Information service	Evacuate inessential staff and all families	On advice (if available)
	Evacuate remainder except volunteers	

Fig. 31. (above and facing page). Crisis flow chart

be dealt with intelligently as they arise. The more comprehensive the plan, the fewer these will be.

The overall responsibility of the committee is to create a climate of confidence, thereby enhancing morale, and at the same time to vigorously dispel fatalistic notions and false rumours which can lead to panic.

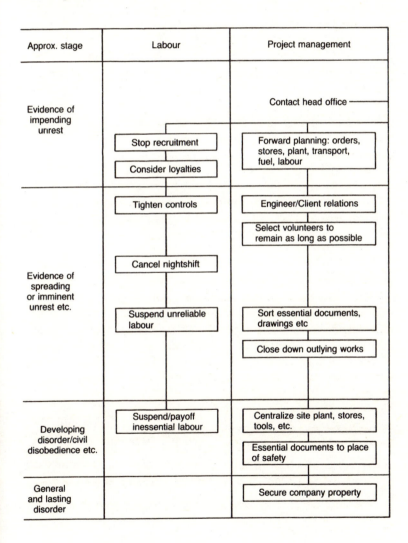

Approx. stage	Labour	Project management
Evidence of impending unrest		Contact head office ———
	Stop recruitment	Forward planning: orders, stores, plant, transport, fuel, labour
	Consider loyalties	
Evidence of spreading or imminent unrest etc.	Tighten controls	Engineer/Client relations
		Select volunteers to remain as long as possible
	Cancel nightshift	
	Suspend unreliable labour	Sort essential documents, drawings etc
		Close down outlying works
Developing disorder/civil disobedience etc.	Suspend/payoff inessential labour	Centralize site plant, stores, tools, etc.
		Essential documents to place of safety
General and lasting disorder		Secure company property

Despite this, there may be some who, although they perform excellently under normal conditions, will feel threatened or frightened and wish to leave the territory in times of crisis. Provided that this is possible, they should not be persuaded to stay against their inclination, as if the situation deteriorates such people can become liabilities and have been known to cause unnecessary panic or alarm.

Figure 31 shows in simple form some of the actions which may have to be taken at the time of impending or actual unrest or disorder. Neither the sequence nor the timing of actions within the arbitrary 'stages' will necessarily be relevant to the particular situation. The chart is solely a guideline.

If it is decided to evacuate the bulk of the expatriate staff to a safer area (possibly in a neighbouring territory), leaving a small number behind to protect company interests, the latter must all be genuine volunteers. They should only be asked to stay when there is no apparent risk to life.

In all cases, actions taken should be in accordance with the recommendations of the nearest UK embassy, high commission or consulate, and actions should be co-ordinated by this office as long as communication can be maintained, provided that the site is not too remote.

Vehicle convoys

There may be occasions when, for protection or otherwise, it is desirable for a number of vehicles to travel in convoy. The following notes generally apply to convoys of five or more vehicles, smaller numbers being much more easily controlled. The essence of good convoy control is to provide security while avoiding unnecessary inconvenience to other road users.

Planning

Route survey. All available routes should, if possible, be reconnoitred beforehand, with particular reference to

- sections which may be impassable to large vehicles or wide loads (e.g. narrow or weak bridges, awkward turns)

- sections which could be difficult or impassable due to rain

- suitable locations for

○ overnight laagers

○ temporary halts

● refuelling facilities

● telephone facilities

● police posts *en route*

● turnings which could be missed or where confusion could arise

● if security is a problem, possible ambush sites.

Police. Whether or not a police escort is planned for all or part of the route, the local police should be advised of the broad intentions and tentative plans. Their advice is usually helpful.

Route selection. Where more than one movement is planned, vary the route if possible, or vary the timings and especially overnight stops, if any. Other things being equal, select the least congested route, even if it is longer.

Movement orders. Prepare a route plan in writing and issue it to all drivers on the day. This should include

● time of departure and estimated times of arrival at designated points on the route

● a clear route plan, with mileages and adequate details such as identification of turnings

● refuelling points

● signals

● action in the event of breakdown or emergency.

The day before the convoy travels, ensure that

● all vehicles have been checked and fuelled

● drivers know what kit, spares and rations to be carried, and where.

On the move

The essential requirements are the following.

● Maintain regulation distance from vehicle in front.

155

- Keep watching vehicle behind in mirror. If it is lagging, slow down. If it disappears, signal vehicle in front.

The drivers of the leading vehicles must remember that the speed required by the rearmost vehicle can be almost twice that of the leading vehicle. Until drivers are experienced, the speed of the lead vehicle should be restricted to 20 mile/h in towns, 30–35 mile/h otherwise.

Spacing. The recommended spacing is 30 vehicles to the mile (VTM) — roughly 50 m between vehicles — closing to 40 VTM (35 m) in towns. Large convoys should travel in blocks (or 'packets') of 4–5 vehicles, with at least 100–150 m between blocks. Ensure that a competent driver is leading each block.

Control. The convoy commander should normally travel in the leading or second vehicle. The second in command should be towards the rear, in a light vehicle (car) which can readily catch up with the leading vehicle. Also at the rear should be a service vehicle: this should be capable of towing any other vehicle and should carry a mechanic, tools, spares, tow bar/chain, etc. The rations and kit vehicle is usually stationed in the centre of a large convoy. Radio communication between the front and rear of a convoy is of great assistance, if available.

Signals. A simple code of signals, thoroughly understood by all drivers, is essential. These can be invented as required. The following are examples

- repeated double flashing of headlamps ($\cdot\cdot$, $\cdot\cdot$, $\cdot\cdot$) 'Slow down'

- continuous flash, driver's arm extended horizontally out of window: 'I have lost the vehicle behind: pass on this signal'

- morse RRR on headlight ($\cdot-\cdot$, $\cdot-\cdot$, $\cdot-\cdot$): 'I am in trouble and stopping'.

Halts. The convoy should be halted for a 15 minute rest break after not more than two hours' continuous driving — if possible at predetermined locations, off the road.

If parked at the roadside, ensure that space is maintained between blocks (or packets) and traffic guides are posted if necessary.

Drivers should check their vehicles and loads at all halts.

At longer halts, vehicles must not be left unattended unless immobilized.

Emergencies: breakdown. In the case of breakdown of a single vehicle, normally the convoy should not stop. The service vehicle should be left to repair the vehicle or take it in tow as appropriate.

It is most important that all drivers know what is expected of them in the event of breakdown of their own vehicle and also of another vehicle.

Emergencies: security protection. If security protection is provided by the police or military authorities, ensure that all personnel are thoroughly conversant with action to be taken in emergency.

Armed protection should normally be situated at the front, at the rear and in the centre of the convoy. Although an experienced ambusher may let part of the convoy through the ambush and cut out the rear section (Nelson style), particular care must be taken when approaching road blocks that vehicles do *not* crowd up nose to tail but maintain standard spacing. Only at routine halts should vehicles be 'waved into' nose to tail formation by someone on the ground.

General practice. The control of large convoys can be more difficult than it first seems. Do not therefore attempt too long a distance with drivers inexperienced in convoy conditions and do not attempt to travel too fast. Be meticulously courteous to other road users. New drivers should be inducted through organized rehearsals.

Care by staff in respect of own security

Expatriate staff can themselves improve their security and that of their dependants, both in their homes and within the local community. General advice includes the following.

- Keep all valuables in a bank or other place of safety, where possible.

- Do not leave any valuables, including passport and traveller's cheques, lying around or in obvious drawers etc.

- Do not wear expensive jewellery or carry more cash than is necessary.

- Keep somebody informed of your whereabouts at all times, so that the management can be informed if you fail to return within a reasonable time.

- Make a note of the whereabouts of the nearest police station, military camps and medical facilities in your area.

- Make a note of your blood group and those of your family. If a blood group is rare, check availability with the nearest hospital.

- Keep a medical pack in your car.

- Cars should be immobilized at night or when left unattended. Steering locks are useful, but may not foil a determined thief.

- Avoid, as far as possible, lonely places and suspect groups.

- Check that the insurance cover for your own personal effects is adequate. If in doubt, obtain advice from personnel department.

- All expatriate staff likely to be resident in the country for several months should register with the nearest high commission, embassy or consulate. This is normally done on your behalf by the management of the company.

Residence security

This section refers to residences not in an expatriate camp but within the local community. Within a camp the security arrangements will be similar to those for buildings and temporary works areas.

Consider adopting at least those security precautions taken by other residents of longer standing in the area.

Examine the residence carefully from the outside and look for weaknesses. But remember that it is a home, not a fortress, and that in most parts of the world potential intruders are usually deterred if they perceive that sensible security measures have been taken and that they are likely to be faced with time-consuming or noisy effort.

Intrusion is usually effected through doors and windows, often with the aid of tools and ladders found on location.

The main exterior door should be stout. It should have a good quality deadlock and either another good lock or a bolt. A spyhole and/or chain will give additional protection.

All other exterior doors should be fitted with internal bolts (top and bottom) especially those to which the servant has a key.

Windows and other openings should be fitted either with bars (minimum 16 mm dia., at 125 mm centres), wire mesh (8 gauge, 60 mm centres) or wrought iron grilles. If the latter, they must be substantial and securely fixed to the surrounds so that they cannot be unscrewed from outside. Wooden shutters (minimum 25 mm timber or 13 mm ply) are a less commonly used substitute and are not so good.

A good perimeter wall or fence is useful for discouraging casual entry. Any thick cover in the garden should be cleared to make a clandestine approach more difficult.

Good lighting during the hours of darkness, both inside and outside the house, is invaluable in deterring intruders. External generators and switch-boxes should be secured. Interior doors should be lockable and locked at night. Windows should also be shut and locked unless there is good reason for not doing so.

In areas of higher risk, it may be useful to keep a whistle and a golf club at one's side during the night. The latter is also useful against snakes. Resistance to armed intruders should only be offered if the resister is very confident of success.

Also in areas of higher risk, it may be good insurance to leave some personal belongings within obvious sight of potential thieves. Small cash, transistor radios, drink etc. can easily be replaced and may discourage the culprit from looking further.

When living in areas remote from other company staff, but not normally in camps, it may be worth considering the use of intruder alarms or, in extreme cases, citizens' band radios. The Project Manager should decide when this is necessary or desirable.

Sophisticated alarm systems have their drawbacks, and should normally only by used in special circumstances.

Barking dogs are in many cases a better deterrent, although there are drawbacks. Rabies is often prevalent. Dogs (and cats) must be vaccinated regularly by the local veterinary officer.

Because of stringent quarantine regulations in the UK, it is an expensive exercise to repatriate a pet and it is often difficult to find a satisfactory home locally. In the event of an unscheduled departure, and a good home not being found, it is essential that the animal is put down to avoid suffering. This must not be shirked. Local vets should generally provide a suitable drug for this purpose in emergencies or should give the required injection.

Care should be taken when employing servants, whose

159

backgrounds should always be checked. Reliance should not be placed on written references (or 'chitties'). Servants should be briefed regularly on security.

Delivery men should not be allowed into the house, and deliveries should be checked before being brought in. Arrangements should be made for repairmen to call by appointment, and their credentials should be checked. Unsolicited gifts and parcels should be refused.

Security guards are most effective when out of sight, although the fact of their presence has a deterrent value. They should be equipped with whistles, torches (but ration and mark all batteries) and possibly a stout stick or pick helve. (It is more usual to expect them to give warning rather than physical protection, but the stick will give them more confidence in challenging intruders.)

Security instructions to servants. A typical check-list of security instructions to servants is as follows.

- Keep all exterior doors closed and locked during the day.

- Keep windows closed when not required to be open.

- At dusk, recheck all exterior doors and windows.

- Do not admit any strangers into the house unless you have been told to expect them. If they say they are repair-men or other company employees, ask for and verify their credentials.

- Do not bring any packages into the house unless you have been told to expect them. Leave them outside (e.g. near the back door) until the householder comes home.

If there is a telephone in the house servants should have the following instructions.

- Do not give information of any kind about the family over the telephone unless you are certain that the caller is a friend. Do not identify either the family or the address to unknown callers.

- If you see anything unusual or suspicious in the vicinity of the house, phone me (or [name]) at the office. Make a note of the registration number of any suspicious car parked near the house and report it to me.

- In any emergency, telephone me at [number] or [name] at [number].

If there is no telephone servants should be told that in the case of emergency they should report the details to [name] making sure the house is properly locked up before they leave.

Cars

All cars should be maintained in good condition, particularly with regard to lights, indicators, mirrors, horn and wipers. In a number of countries, police or army checks are not infrequent and it is desirable not to give any excuse for being stopped and checked if it can be avoided.

Cars should be immobilized at night or when parked unattended, particularly in city centres. Steering locks are useful, but not an absolute deterrent to a determined thief.

Do not leave attractive items (camera, clothes, bags etc.) visible within the car, even if it is locked.

When travelling, keep doors locked and do not leave windows open more than is necessary for comfort.

Be particularly alert when approaching

- a road block — look early for signs that it is a genuine police block

- an accident; particularly a solitary body lying on the road — slow down and be prepared to stop beyond the accident/body; in some countries it is desirable in any event to drive on and report the circumstances at the next police post.

In remote areas, especially after dark, or if carrying cash or other valuables, it is advisable to travel in company whenever possible.

If you are allocated a personal driver, ensure that his character and qualifications have been verified.

Kidnapping and terrorist activity

Successful assassination or kidnapping is invariably achieved only after careful planning. The plan would be formulated after meticulous reconnaissance of the target in order to establish his routine, habits and vulnerable points. A potential target who is aware of the threat and takes sensible countermeasures will normally be abandoned for easier alternatives.

Protect your house, your family and yourself as indicated in the previous sections.

CONSTRUCTION IN DEVELOPING COUNTRIES

You are very vulnerable when on the move, and probably at your most vulnerable when entering or leaving your home. At these times be always alert, suspicious and aware of anything unusual. Look well ahead to cars parked along the road, and in the rear mirror for anything suspicious. Be prepared to postpone a move, or drive past your destination, if (for example) you see two or three men loitering in a car nearby. If you believe you are being followed, drive to the nearest police or military post or other 'safe' establishment.

Make a habit of examining the street outside before you leave any building.

Vary your routes and timings. This is probably the greatest single contribution that can be made to good personal security.

Do not stop immediately behind any car in a lonely road, thereby blocking your escape route.

Do not leave your car unattended if you can avoid it. Keep it in a locked garage, never on the road outside your house.

Try to assume a low-profile image. Avoid publicity, particularly press photographs.

Ensure that your family adopt, as far as possible, the measures outlined above.

Civil disorder, coups, and riots

The first rule in any sort of political, military or civil disturbance is to *keep your head down*. If you are at home, stay there. If you are out, get home or to site as quickly as you reasonably can, avoiding as far as possible main centres and troubled areas.

Do not panic. Time spent thinking is usually well spent. Make a plan. If you have to move, move quickly but circumspectly. If possible, be where the management expect you to be. You could cause unnecessary trouble and risk rushing off to some hiding place nobody else knows about.

When the opportunity arises, make contact with the company, or other staff in the area. If at home, wait for instructions. The company usually has a plan, albeit a flexible one, for emergencies. Its first concern is for *your* safety. Do not hinder it by acting independently, but at the same time take reasonable precautions to protect yourself and your family.

It is useful to listen to the radio, both the local stations and the BBC Overseas Service if you can, but be careful and be sceptical of everything you hear. Even the latter has, on occasion, relayed garbage. Do not pass on unsubstantiated rumours.

If the nuisance looks like being protracted, immediately conserve food supplies and water. Carry your passport, cash and any important documents on your person, or at least have them handy.

Pack one small but strong suitcase with essential items (clothing, toiletries, shoes) but bear in mind that you and your family must be able to *hand carry* all the luggage you propose to take in the event of a hasty departure, still leaving one hand free.

Guns

Any type of gun, sporting or other, poses a potential risk both to the owner and to the community. Therefore the approval of the Project Manager is essential before any type of gun is retained on property owned or leased by the company. The Project Manager must satisfy himself that satisfactory arrangements are made for the safe and secure storage of both gun and ammunition when not in use, and should impose such safeguards as he considers necessary. Also the restrictions concerning the importation and licensing of guns and ammunition must be thoroughly investigated and rigidly adhered to.

Permission to keep a personal firearm should only be granted under the most exceptional circumstances, and the firearm should only be carried when there is real danger to life.

Before keeping a personal firearm, you must first satisfy the Project Manager that you are competent both to handle it and to look after it responsibly, and you must also make the personal decision that you would be prepared to use it to take life (if your own was in danger) — even, if necessary, that of a young woman. If you are less determined, the firearm can only increase the danger to yourself.

Resistance to armed intruders should only be offered if you are very confident of success. If you have any reservations whatsoever about keeping a gun — whether a pistol or a 12 bore — don't keep one.

12 Commissioning and demobilizing

The commissioning and demobilizing period includes the contractual maintenance liabilities for remedying defects.

The extent of commissioning liabilities will vary depending on the complexity of the project. In the case of a road, it may involve a simple inspection and handover procedure. This will be made more complicated if road maintenance and traffic management are included.

A power project will usually require a complex series of tests run on load.

In a developing country, the procedure may be complicated by the need to train the facility operating staff at the same time, and by the lack of input and output connections and feeds. The training programme itself may extend the commissioning period.

It is not the intention here to discuss the normal testing and commissioning-test procedures that would apply in any country, but only to draw attention to the problems that can occur in the Third World. These problems may, among other matters, concern

- availability of trained operating staff
- fuel supplies
- capability of existing system to accept the output
- visas for commissioning staff
- spares for defects
- communications.

As with most things in the developing world, commissioning may have a political dimension, and the timing of the tests will have to be determined well in advance.

The procedure for the discharge of warranties and release from liability and associated insurance should be part of the demobilization programme. The requirement for the Client to insure the plant from a particular date should be clearly established. Though contractually the liability may be deemed to pass on to the Client on a particular date, measures should be taken to prevent any gap occurring in the insurance of the project.

Before the commissioning tests start, a pre-commissioning programme should be carried out to check the procedure and instruct the staff who will carry out and observe the tests. This should also ensure that all the necessary equipment has been assembled.

At the time of completion of a hydroelectric project, the lack of river flow or storage or the failure of others to complete the delivery system required for any type of power scheme may restrict the scope of the completion tests that can be run. Nevertheless, a restricted set of tests should be carried out and handover should be accomplished subject to the undertaking of any remedial measures which may be found necessary when the final tests are completed.

The problems of demobilization are similar to those of mobilization, but in reverse. If there is no further work for the company within the territory, demobilization is a *de facto* evacuation. Under these circumstances, the demobilization plan must be carefully prepared and rehearsed well in advance. The factors to be taken into consideration are

- reduction in the European expatriate staff

- pay-off of the labour force

- allocation of work to subcontractors

- discharge of fiscal and legal obligations

- re-export of construction plant

- settlement of final account with the Client.

Reduction in European staff

Repatriation of staff will have tax implications for the individuals concerned and this must be taken into consideration when the rota is decided. Generally, to be free of tax complications at home the expatriates must have completed at least one year of absence abroad.

The wind-down procedure will result in dependants being sent home before the end of the contract. Ideally, this operation should be completed by at least three months before the end. As far as possible, timing should suit re-entry into the home education system for the children, and this will usually involve the return also of the wives of staff members. The first staff to be reduced should be production staff. Plant maintenance staff should be retained to prepare the plant for resale. Stores staff will be involved in packing up for re-export or local sale. The final element of senior staff to return home will be the commercial staff involved in the settlement of the final account with the Client.

After handover has been completed, the commercial manager or chief quantity surveyor is usually made the project manager and he usually remains in the territory during the defects-liability period. By the end of this, he should have achieved final settlement of the account. Under him there will probably remain one member of European staff to supervise the subcontractors or skeleton labour force still retained for remedial or maintenance work.

The expatriate camp should normally be retained until commissioning is complete, in order to house commissioning staff. Thereafter, it should be dismantled or disposed of. The remaining commercial staff are likely to need to transfer to the location of the Client's main office. The liaison office is likely to be retained during this period and be the only office within the territory. All files and records in the territory should be sent to the liaison office and kept there until that closes down.

The final discharge of fiscal and legal obligations in the territory may take some time after settlement of the final account. The liaison office, with all its records, may have to be retained for this period under the control of a local member of staff or an appointed part-time representative. Questions that may arise during this period may have to be answered by visitors from the home base, temporarily using the liaison office and its documents.

Arrangements should be made for work permits to be released and tax clearance completed so that staff who were previously resident can operate as occasional visitors where necessary. In some countries, foreign personnel have difficulty in getting visitors' visas within one year of giving up residence or work permits.

Pay-off of the labour force

The discharge of labour can be complicated in some countries. The retention of the best workers to the last may not be possible. Political considerations will prevail, and normally workers from the immediate locality will have to be retained longest, even if they do not have the appropriate skills.

The demobilization plan must be discussed well in advance with the local labour office. Some form of compensation for loss of job may be involved. Alternatively, if there are other projects in the locality, it may be difficult to retain an adequate labour force to the end once the job is seen to be passing its peak. Under these circumstances, it may be possible to make arrangements with the Client to have some of the labour force eventually transferred to any maintenance and operations facility that the Client will have after project completion.

Whichever is the case, a plan should be formulated to transfer a number of activities to subcontractors during the close-down phase.

Where the labour force consists of third-country nationals, the contracts must provide for a progressive repatriation of labour. Work permits and labour may be transferable to other employers in the territory.

Discharge of fiscal and legal obligations

Legal and fiscal matters that have to be dealt with during the close-down period include

- individual expatriate tax clearances

- company tax clearance

- discharge of all obligations as a local employer

- payment of duty on plant and materials retained in the territory or obtainment of release of bonds posted against the re-export of such items (if the contract is fully duty-paid, these matters are not relevant)

- determination of all contracts with local parties

- termination of insurances

- obtainment of return of bonds.

Re-export of construction plant and surplus materials

How the re-export of construction plant and surplus materials is dealt with depends on the nature of the contract: whether it is or is not duty free.

If it is duty free there will be an obligation to re-export, and this may be enforced by bonds which were given when the plant was originally imported. If such items are sold locally the company will usually be penalized by having duty levied, based on original imported value, including freight cost. If the sale is to be to another duty-free contract, it may be possible to rearrange the paperwork to allow this to happen. However, this may introduce insurmountable complications.

The paperwork associated with the re-export of plant must be carefully correlated with the information in the original import documentation. Even the most minor discrepancy is likely to delay the re-export or result in penalties. The Author has knowledge of one situation where a large machine entered a country in one piece. For re-export it was broken down into several elements to suit a smaller vessel. In the end, this method of re-export had to be abandoned because the paperwork could not be made acceptable to the authorities.

Spare parts may present difficulties in duty-free situations. The substituted parts may themselves have to be re-exported. Normally it is simpler to have the spare parts on a duty-paid basis, even where the plant is duty-free. However, as shown in chapter 10, spare parts can be as much as 150% of the capital value of some machines on a long-duration project, and the cost penalty of paying duty on these could be onerous.

On long-duration contracts, it is normal to sell the plant at the end of the contract period. In the absence both of buyback agreements with suppliers and of local sales possibilities, it is usual to send the plant to international auctions, which are held regularly in a number of venues. Arrangements for this need to be made well in advance and the plant will have to be brought to a saleable state. The cost of this and the freight to the port of sale has to be reconciled with the anticipated sale value.

Settlement of final account

The settlement of the final account with the Client is normally the last activity on a contract.

The settlement of the final account and the attendant release of retention monies and bonds can be a long drawn out affair in some countries. Normally this will require the retention of records and the presence of commercial staff in the territory until well after effective completion of the project. While these final details are being settled, it is important to ensure that no gap opens out in the insurance of the project.

The company's agent for the project will normally have to assist during this period. His agreement should therefore contain sufficient incentive for his assistance to be effective.

Glossary and abbreviations

Glossary

Agent
: Used in the general sense of a representative, either a company or an individual, who has some authority, specified through a written agreement, to commit a company

Client
: The Employer, owner or promoter of a project

The Engineer
: The person named in a contract to instruct and supervise the contractor

Indent
: An internal requisition to initiate the purchasing of materials or the appointment of a subcontractor

Project Manager
: The contractor's manager in charge of the project and authorized representative in the territory

Vendor
: A supplier of materials and equipment which are to be installed by a construction contractor

Abbreviations

ECGD
: Export Credits Guarantee Department (HM Government)

E&M
: Electrical and mechanical

FOB
: Free on board ship (delivery of goods)

GE
: General expenses

ODA
: Overseas Development Administration

QS
: Quantity surveyor

Bibliography

Boeva B. Management of joint international projects. *International Journal of Project Management*, 1990, **8**, May, No. 2, 105–108.

Fan L. Equity joint ventures in the Chinese construction industry. *International Journal of Project Management*, 1988, **6**, Feb., No. 1, 50–58.

Hayes R.W. *et al. Risk management in engineering construction*. Science and Engineering Research Council and Thomas Telford, London, 1986.

Institution of Civil Engineers. *Management of international construction projects*. Thomas Telford, London, 1985.

Institution of Civil Engineers. *Overseas projects — crucial problems*. Thomas Telford, London, 1988.

International Construction Law Review, 1990, **7**, part 3. Three papers on turnkey plant contracts.

Merna A. and Smith N.J. Project managers and the use of turnkey contracts. *International Journal of Project Management*, 1990, **8**, Aug., No. 3, 183–189.

Sawyer J.G. and Gillott C.A. *FIDIC digest: contractual claims and responsibilities under the fourth edition of the FIDIC conditions*. Thomas Telford, London, 1990.

Stallworthy E.A. and Kharbanda O.P. *International construction and the role of project management*. Gower Press, London, 1985.

Stuckenbruck L.C. and Zomorrodian A. Project management: the promise for developing countries. *International Journal of Project Management*, 1987, **5**, Aug., No. 3, 167–175.

Thompson P.A. and Perry J.G. *Operation of the target cost contract for the construction of the Makambako–Wino road, Tanzania*, final report on Phase I, 1984, and report on Phase II, 1987. Overseas Development Administration, London.

Woodward D.G. *et al.* Build–own–operate–transfer (BOOT) contracts. *Project* (Association of Project Managers), 1991, Apr., 28–30.